Editorial

Troubling gestures and postures have been on display recently, urgent-seeming causes, burning-seeming issues, that insist on speaking but dare not quite speak their name. They have political or ideological implications but avoid direct statement. To declare is to distort, they imply. Signals familiar to initiates are used. All will be revealed in time, they say. Meanwhile, we are left in the dark.

On 26 January fellows and honorary fellows of the Royal Society of Literature received an email signed jointly by the Chair and the Director of the RSL which began, 'We are aware of a concerted campaign of disinformation concerning the RSL and our *Review* magazine.' As a fellow, I was not aware of a campaign. 'We strongly refute the false narrative being presented via emails and social media posts. We ask that you refrain from sharing this misinformation yourselves.' Disinformation, misinformation: are they synonymous? 'The RSL's Council meets next month [i.e., in February] to discuss this matter, and to consider next steps regarding the damaging and false claims made.' Of course, I immediately set out to uncover the occasion for this email.

In the four opaque email paragraphs that followed, there were clues – 'this matter' seemed to entail alleged censorship, the spiking of an article in the RSL *Review*, a delay in the publication itself, the dismissal of the seven-year, generally admired editor Maggie Ferguson. These allegations seemed substantial, and perhaps substantiated. Was it the case that the RSL's leadership was reluctant, despite pressure from some fellows, formally to stand by Salman Rushdie after his injuries in the knife attack? Discussion 'was closed down by the leadership, according to some who attended'.

The RSL insisted that an explanation would follow, the allegedly spiked article would appear. The delay had to do with reformatting... 'The magazine is the only publication the RSL puts out annually – we want it to be the best it can be, and to speak to the widest possible audience. We therefore decided to move it forward to a new format and style that better reflects, and includes, our Fellowship and allows more space for conversations among them, and with other writers.' I learned that the RSL was in the midst of a 'wider brand refresh'. (When I was asked to join, I didn't think the RSL was a brand.) It appointed a 'new Communications team' late in 2023. May it soon communicate.

On 27 January, a day after fellows received the email, the *Guardian* announced that 'a major revolt among longer-term fellows is now threatening to destabilise the society. A council meeting of members next month will be forced to address a growing number of complaints.' Some of those complaints began to clarify the RSL's insistence that the magazine had to 'better reflect, and include' the new members of the fellowship. Marina Warner, a previous RSL president, told the *Observer*, 'It is a question of a lack of respect for older members and a loss of institutional history, which was something fellows cherished.' A new fellow exclaimed, 'The society should not just be for a group of older, rather entitled, people, however distinguished. These problems had to be sorted quickly.'

Bernardine Evaristo, the RSL's current president, insists that the society, far from being old-fashioned, is 'very forward-looking, very progressive and committed to inclusion at every level'. Certainly it has ticked boxes to receive increased public subsidy. Some members are less sanguine than their president, however. The *Observer* reported, 'The novelist and biographer Miranda Seymour recently resigned, and amid allegations of "scandalous" disregard for proper procedures, a number of members have told the *Observer* they are considering following suit. This comes after the resignation in 2018 of Piers Paul Read in response to an initial call for younger fellows.' Other 'allegations' are not specified. Evaristo is clear: the RSL should be 'for all writers, rather than traditionally writers who are white and middle class'.

The attempt to redress that imbalance resulted in sixty-two new fellows being inducted in 2023; changes to the ways members are recruited are proposed. 'Currently, to be recognised with fellowship an author must be nominated by an existing fellow or honorary fellow before being considered by the RSL council and senior officers. Under the new process the public will be invited to recommend writers for fellowship and then a series of broader-based election panels will consider the recommendations. This is the sort of fundamental switch that unsettles writer Amanda Craig: "It used to be an enormous honour to become a fellow. But when people are just starting their writing careers, it is not the same."' Anne Chisholm, quondam chair, told the *Observer*: 'Of course the RSL, like all venerable institutions, has an imperfect past: it needed to change with the times. My worry is that the pace and style of change has lately been alienating too many fellows and disrespecting the RSL's history.'

Marina Warner did not resign despite unease with the direction the RSL is taking. She supports efforts to broaden the fellowship. 'There were of course a lot of old, white liberals like me, for historical reasons, and while I was president we launched a drive to lower the average age. The problem is a fellowship used to mark an acclaimed career.' She added, 'And I was very disappointed too that we did not stand up more for Salman. It should have been nothing to do with his views, or even necessarily admiring his work.'

Bernardine Evaristo declared in the *Guardian* on 8 February that 'no single group or demographic within the fellowship should feel they own' the RSL. She insisted that it would have been improper for the RSL to make a public stand for Rushdie: 'It cannot take sides in writers' controversies and issues' – as though there were two sides to an attempted knife murder on a writer, whoever that writer, or murderer, might be. If such are what Evaristo describes as the 'governance protocols' of the fellowship, they were not explained to me when I was ceremoniously inducted and signed the book with George Orwell's pen.

This editorial was written before news of the RSL's annual general meeting and its outcomes broke in the news and on social media.

Letters to the editor

Coleridge redivivus

Jeremy Hooker writes: I am writing to thank you for your editorial in *PNR* 275. Your quotation from Christopher Middleton is one that I cherish. Following my first essay on his work, in *PNR* [114, 1997], Christopher wrote to me, initiating a correspondence between us over several years. I don't know whether he saved my letters, but I kept all of his. I always thought of Christopher as the equal of Coleridge for our time. Of course, he was very 'modern' (alive in and to our time) and more playful than STC!

Who loves, raves

Rory Waterman writes: Recently, on Twitbook or whatever it's called, Gregory Woods drew attention to a passage in Jeffrey Meyers's review of Andrew Stauffer, *Byron: A Life in Ten Letters* (*PNR* 275), in which Hemingway (1899–1961) is referred to as 'the Byron of our time'. I suppose they both liked bears.

It isn't the only bizarre claim Meyers has been permitted to make. I puzzled over the declaration that Byron's clubfoot 'chained his dull spirit to the proud earth', and wondered how this tallies with the perhaps justified assertion that he 'had the most fascinating character and life of any British poet', and the wholly justified one that 'with fire, passion and wit he made world history'. I pondered over the notion of Lady Caroline Lamb having 'poured lava through his veins', though at least here I knew what he meant. Then I pondered another while over the suggestion (and attendant image) that 'English society was saturated in sodomy', and had a few other little ponders between and either side, my eyebrows and jaw growing ever more distant.

In this context, it is perhaps unfortunate that Meyers fastidiously points out three typos that 'should be corrected'. I hugely admire *PNR* for its unfashionable commitment to being a broad church of styles and perspectives, but giving the author freedom to publish such wild comments in your pages feels a bit like letting a toddler play on the stairs. Perhaps there was no need to fit a safety gate, but a little more adult supervision wouldn't have gone amiss.

Corrections

Jasmina Bolfek-Radovani writes: I am writing to point to a couple of factual errors in the review of my multilingual poetry collection *Knitting drum machines for exiled tongues* by Oliver Dixon in *PNR* 274. I was sorry to read in the second sentence of the second paragraph that the reviewer attributed my place of birth to Serbia. I was born in Zagreb, the capital city of Croatia; I was not born in Serbia. Serbia and Croatia each has its own language, identity and culture, although they share a common, complex history.

The third sentence of the review mentions that *Knitting drum machines for exiled tongues* is my first collection instead of being my second one. This can be verified by going to my website page: https://jasminabradovani.com/pages/poetry-collection-reveries-about-language.

Oliver Dixon replies: Really sorry for the slips. I can only attribute them to human error/mental errancy.

News & Notes

The American South loses a substantial Man of Letters • Fred Chappell wrote novels and lyric poetry out of the life of North Carolina's Appalachian Piedmont region. He died in January at the age of eighty-seven. An heir to Faulkner, Flannery O'Connor, Robert Penn Warren and Eudora Welty, he was also a significant critical voice. His poetry – eighteen collections – is rooted in the elegiac tones and clarity of Welty. He also wrote a dozen novels and two volumes of criticism. In 1985 he shared the Bollingen Prize with John Ashbery.

Like Ashbery, he took bearings from European modernism, though he did not share Ashbery's inventiveness or humour. Most of his life was spent in North Carolina, with a formative nine-month Rockefeller Foundation-funded stay in Florence in 1967–8. His poems registered the collision between a rural tradition and the rapid transformations of an encroaching urban present – the challenge to values and to forms. *The Times* obituarist wrote, 'He revelled in the subtle sophistication of agrarian ways, in the artistry of a sampler quilt and the architectural genius of a century-old barn, and he understood that the way of life that made them possible was fast crumbling.' His poetry and prose harmonised in his verse quartet *Midquest* (1981) and a quartet of novels written between the 1970s and 1990s. *I Am One of You Forever* (1987) is probably his fiction masterpiece.

His poems often meditate on the experiences of women, finding space in an inferred reality; and then, without them, it alters:

The rooms were quiet when she was resident.
Now they lie silent. That is different.

A poet ally of Navalny removed • Lev Rubinstein, a supporter of Alexei Navalny and an outspoken critic of Putin and of the war in Ukraine, known as a poet dissident and essayist before Putin and during his protracted presidency, was struck by a car and killed in Moscow. He was seventy-six. In 2004 he declared, 'Today's Russia has no place for free citizens and independent poets. [...] It barrels through them, not stopping at the red light to see them cross the road.' It proved an ironic prophesy of his own death. He was a founder of the Russian conceptualism movement, the obituaries said, 'an avant-garde fusion of art and prose that thumbed its nose at the restrictions of the Socialist Realism that predominated in the 1970s and '80s.'

In 1999 he received the first independent literary prize, the Andrei Bely for poetry that rejects censorship. He was also a novelist. 'He was a living legend,' said Boris Filanovsky, who wrote an opera based on Rubinstein's works that premiered in 2011. 'His texts concern the very matter of language – what we say in Russia now seems to be stolen from Rubinstein's texts.' The social media response to his death was widespread.

Surveillance Cameras • Some American friends have been doing weekend work at an independent bookshop. It was surprising, they said, to see a sign posted in the history section advising customers that a surveillance camera had been installed. This was because books on Palestinian and Jewish history, but especially Palestinian, had been despoiled – back covers and pages torn out, etc. Such vandalism, targeting an independent bookshop in a mixed and diverse community: what outcome does it seek?

A great publisher revives • It was announced on 24 January that Christopher MacLehose, one of the most inventive publishers of the last fifty years, will be launching Open Borders Press at Orenda Books. Karen Sullivan, Publisher of Orenda Books, announced that MacLehose will lead Orenda's first-ever imprint. MacLehose's Mountain Leopard Press list was sold by Welbeck to Hachette in December 2022. He will now publish Open Borders Press as an associate list of Orenda Books.

Having commissioned translations from thirty-seven languages during his years as a publisher, MacLehose will continue to champion authors of exceptional quality from all over the world. The list hopes to match the success of the Harvill Press (established by him) and MacLehose Press, publishing the best literary fiction and non-fiction, much of it in translation. The quality of the translations and of every aspect of the design of the books will (as in the past) be paramount. Koukla MacLehose, who founded the celebrated scouting agency that bore her name, will work with the Press. The first Open Borders Press title, Andrey Kurkov's *Our Daily War*, a sequel to the international bestselling *Diary of an Invasion*, will be published in the summer.

The Poetry Translation Centre turns twenty • As part of its celebrations – which will include an ambitious events programme and a poetry prize – the PTC are publishing a substantial collection of essays, poems and letters by established international poets, including Yang Lian, Bejan Matur, Diana Bellessi and Habib Tengour. *Living in Language* is a valuable resource for poets and readers of poetry. It is scheduled for 7 March.

The book also contains fascinating correspondence between Diana Bellessi and Ursula Le Guin. The lyric essays, fragments, letters and new poems that emerge in this anthology will shed light on topics, we are told, such as 'writing the body, writing in exile, writing as witness, writing as a shamanic act, grappling with traditional forms, discovering your own voice, and even translation and self- translation'. The editor of the book is Erica Hesketh.

Peepal Tree Press and HopeRoad Publishing merge • Peepal Tree Press and HopeRoad Publishing, from the first of February, are joining forces. They see in each other companies with a compatible ethos, backlists and complementary publishing identities. Peepal Tree will take responsibility for the production of HopeRoad's titles, marketing and back-office operations. HopeRoad will retain ownership and control of its IP and its choices of new titles. This process should run smoothly because both Peepal Tree and HopeRoad are represented by Inpress Ltd and distributed by BookSource. HopeRoad will be developing five new titles to add to Peepal Tree's sixteen scheduled for 2024.

Peepal Tree is an independent, specialist publisher of Caribbean and Black British titles, including fiction, poetry and non-fiction. Founded in 1985, it has published over 450 books, including Costa, T.S. Eliot, Forward, OCM Bocas, Guyana and Casa de las Americas prize winners. Jeremy Poynting leads it, with operations manager Hannah Bannister. Its associate editor for poetry is Kwame Dawes. HopeRoad was founded in 2010 by Rosemarie Hudson. Her emphasis has been to promote writing from and about Africa, Asia and the Caribbean. Rosemarie was joined in 2019 by Pete Ayrton, founder of Serpent's Tail.

Authors are investing their writing in Substack • Seven years from the publishing platform's launch, Substack is helping many writers 'break through the noise' and build a readership that can answer back, without forfeiting rights to their work. Fiction writers feature, but so do poets, poetry critics and readers. A spokesperson for Substack says, 'most readers only stay in touch with the writers they love through the books they publish, at best, every few years. Substack enables them to have a constant dialogue with their favourite authors, understanding their thoughts and ideas beyond the novels they write.'

We invite readers to contribute advocacies of Substack poets and critics with whom they regularly engage. Among the poets I subscribe to are Zohar Atkins, Jeremy Noel-Tod, Victoria Moul… And *PN Review* itself has a lively Substack account.

Paula Modersohn-Becker • Michael Augustin writes: I wanted to let your readers know that there will be a spectacular exhibition of paintings by Paula Modersohn-Becker in New York at Neue Galerie / New Gallery and at The Art Institute of Chicago this year.
https://www.neuegalerie.org/
Art Institute of Chicago https://g.co/kgs/nuJ1Qor

Moving in Time

ANTHONY VAHNI CAPILDEO

Listen! Something marvellous happened in the middle of the night when noisy folk had shut up and gone to bed. The Old English poet in *The Dream of the Rood* has to tell you about it. Fabulous and gleaming, then smeared with blood and sweat, the Cross on which Christ was crucified is appearing to him, one way then another, steadily but in flashes. It continues to stand steadfast, continues alternately to shine with glory or drip with gore, while telling the poet how it grew up: its innocent tree-childhood, one among many in the wood; being singled out, cut down, and carried away by the men who turned it into an instrument of torture; being put in the position of killing the young hero stretched on it dreadfully, desirously embracing him though it killed. The flashes troubled me. They reminded me of what my father suffered: obsessive images of harm occurring to his family, images of himself doing that harm. In my late teens, at university, I found ways to write about the poem that left out affect. But things on pages continued to move.

Before you enter the deep bath, roofed with a canopy of stars, you have begun to feel a change. Bodies in motion and leaping flame are reflected in polished metal, showing or casting shadows on the glitter moss of mosaic. They seem to metamorphose. Creature, you feel part of creation as process. So, at least, my friend Mike – theologian, classicist, puppeteer and trained clown – explained to me how Christian baptism in the ancient world perhaps partook of a sensibility not alien to earlier men afraid of being turned into deer, women desperate to become trees, and in-between genders blowing like windflowers. Dying to the old life and entering the new was a break, but not a discontinuity. I think this is what Mike said. The immersion in movement, openness to being moved, troubled me.

Mike and I are working with a dancer. The dancer creates a score in two parts, displayed on two walls in the studio. One charts and lists wounds from the *Iliad*, with helpful diagrams of human anatomy. Another cues us into gesture. Mike and I stand in the corner, looking from wall to wall, before stepping out onto the black floor. As part of the rehearsal process, one of us reads portions of Emily Wilson's *Iliad* translation aloud, over and over. The other two move. This is discombobulating for me, despite my previous experiments in immersive theatre. Surely you don't do that to Homer? Certainly not with a fluffy seal puppet among the props... Reading Great Literature contemporary-leisure-style can assume the privilege of stillness. You sit with the text, and its difficulty (emotional, linguistic, other). You turn it as you contemplate it as a surface of words; you notice areas of brightness for you, highlight them further, focus more closely, take some distance, reckon with the strange. You are the still (small) point that contains the words' (immense) turning world. It does not matter if you are in bed with the book, or if you have left the book, or screen, behind, to walk or roll with the text in memory, waiting on bleachers or in hospital or in a queue in the late-night shop; nonetheless, you become, and benefit from, the stillness around the text or textual fragment. 'Walking poetry' workshops, or taking a poem outdoors, need not at all disturb the relationship between reader and text. You are in charge, becoming the fortress-husk in which the poem germinates. You are not necessarily open to change. This is not so if you are a body in motion in a procession, yourself image and acted-upon.

I do wonder if dismissal of some poetry (like my beloved Martin Carter's) as 'political' comes from the fear of *being amongst*, the fear of being changed, the distrust of speech that can pass from mouth to mouth; the valorization of silent reading as golden, reading aloud as common coin, chanting as some kind of emotional scam. Yet... who says that a poem about being alone in nature at sunset feeling heterosexually in love is political? Nobody; yet that lyrical, uncontroversial, able-bodied, very likely masculine poetic persona is not behaving as many safety-conscious ciswomen would, and almost certainly not in a war zone. I would argue that there is no more political poem than the one where the speaker is enjoying peace. The margins of such a poem are a charge sheet at the rest of the world's expense, even if the text embodies a beauty or serenity that everyone deserves. It is acceptable to envisage classical wounds in a university setting. Homer, like Shakespeare, is permissible. People who would put down political poetry will make the face they make when something good is happening in the culture. They will not be moved.

Martin Carter opens 'Black Friday 1962':

were some who ran one way.
were some who ran another way.

were some who did not run at all.
were some who will not run again.
and I was with them all [...]

Reading, I notice physical changes in myself, and personal upset. I can imagine the people in those streets, closely, looking like my neighbours that I grew up with, lit by a similar phase of sunlight. Is it because the context is 'relatable', Caribbean – even though I have never been to Guyana? Is it because the words not only describe movement, and disrupt grammar, but themselves have a quality of being in motion, phrase passing to phrase like something in the streets (a pamphlet or a ragged banner or a bandage or a quick breath), barely passing between the event of dispersal and violence, and the event of the poem? There seems hardly a pause for the poet to have collected words and formed them in his imagination. Yet... he did, not without art.

The poet of *The Dream of the Rood* uses a triple technique to induce us to hear (or read) feelingly: the flashing of alternate images, each distinct, an overlay in memory but never a palimpsest; a life story, where the Rood reassures us that it has emotional agency despite being literally displaced, fixed and bound; and the as-if-natural intertwining of heroic imagery (culturally familiar to his audience) with Christian religious language (comparatively foreign). It strikes me that, while this triple technique draws on the visual, its effectiveness arises from how it 'messes with' our relation to time. The religious event happens (continues happening) over three days and also in time eternal; the tree's lifespan is of uncertain years, but certainly years rather than days; the flashing images hit the mind at midnight and keep flashing.

Carter can be dismissed as political, not lyrical; the Old English poet can be pigeonholed as devotional; more important for me, as a practitioner of the craft and also as a human creature, is how both texts *move*; they are in motion, and they are moving. Looking at a crucifix on the wall, it would be a mistake to see the serenity and beauty of a yogi, or an Apollonian athlete, at full and birdlike stretch. It is essential to look with eyes of time. The image is not static but agonizing. The core strains as gravity pulls the body earthwards; every muscle is working against the fall and against bondage; the nerves are in overdrive. We have forgotten, as readers who like good things happening in the culture, to look with the eyes of time; whether at the poem, always politically on the page, or at the child under rubble, heir to a lineage, seeded with long life.

AI and Poetry

ROBERT GRIFFITHS

Unlike the opaquely named ChatGPT (what does that do then?), Google's Artificial Intelligence (AI) chatbot, Bard, hints at the jobs and the people it might replace: writing jobs, and poets, for example.

Jonathan Swift knew this was coming three hundred years ago. He imagined, in *Gulliver's Travels,* a wooden word-permutator, 'the engine', and how it would take over writing: 'Every one knew how laborious the usual method is of attaining to arts and sciences; whereas, by his contrivance, the most ignorant person, at a reasonable charge, and with a little bodily labour, might write books in philosophy, poetry, politics, laws, mathematics, and theology, without the least assistance from genius or study.'

And it has started, with A-level students already ditching expensive Pearson study guides for AI generated revision notes, knocking £1bn off the publisher's share price. The rats are leaving the rising ship with Geoffrey Hinton, one of Google's AI moguls, resigning with an ominous graveside warning: 'Right now, they're not more intelligent than us, as far as I can tell. But I think they soon may be.'

In many ways they clearly are, and have been for a while. The recently crowned world chess champion, Ding Liren, has a rating of 2,789. The best chess computer, Stockfish, is 3,500. No contest. Pets are also in trouble, with Furby – 'The more you play with me, the more I do' – offering what no dog can offer.

So how do poets stand? It doesn't look good. Asked to produce a love poem, Bard started off with:

I love the way you make me laugh,
Even when I don't feel like it.
I love the way you always know
How to make me feel better.

Similarly invited, Shakespeare threw in what he said was his 116th sonnet, ending with the slightly dubious:

Love alters not with his brief hours and weeks,
But bears it out even to the edge of doom.
If this be error and upon me proved,
I never writ, nor no man ever loved.

Asked whether he had sought computer assistance here, the poet stomped off, leaving the matter unresolved.

Presumably a poet, Bard included, is enriched through the work of other poets. Asked to produce something in the manner of Seamus Heaney, Bard offered us lines which included:

I work with a pen.
My hands are soft and white.
I write about the land,
But I have never worked it.

Heaney himself, when invited to produce something on the same lines, came up with verses that included the obviously inferior:

The coarse boot nestled on the lug, the shaft
Against the inside knee was levered firmly.
He rooted out tall tops, buried the bright edge deep
To scatter new potatoes that we picked,
Loving their cool hardness in our hands.

One to zero to Bard, we thought.

Leaving the room, Heaney started to rant at us along the lines that poems weren't just 'arrangements of words'. He said *his* poem had let down 'a shaft into real life'. His last words, as the door slammed, was that 'it' – we assume he was characterising Bard's effort – was 'a big coarse-grained navvy of a poem'. He has some brass.

SET 3: Mondo de Dormo

TRANSLATED BY JOHN GALLAS

1
Sleepless Ise no Taifu early eleventh century/Japan

Sleepless... tired of thinking...
turn over... and look dumbly out at my dark garden –
to see some careless hand meantimes
has lighted lines of dew along the cabbageheads.

2
I come from foggy, faroff lands... Amado Nervo 1870–1919/Mexico

I come from foggy, faroff lands.
The king is old, the king is sad.
My soul seeks only what is strange.
My soul loves what cannot be had.

You weep for dreams a world away.
You wait on loves that will not come.
Your eyes are sleepy, wet and wild,
like wind-dipped wings; your heart is numb.

Ah, both of us were born the same –
still seeking what cannot be had:
that foggy, faroff country where
the king is old, the king is sad.

3
Lullaby Anonymous (undated)/Myanmar

on the moon's round cay
a gold hare squats
nip-eyed
nip-eyed
sleep now... sleep now... sleep

an old bone man
is mashing rice
on the moon's round cay
so sleep... sleep... sleep

the Nats are dancing
on the moon's round cay
tree-high
tree-high
sleep now... sleep now... sleep

an old red sun
is painting your eyes
hush now and shut them
and sleep... sleep... sleep

4

Tomorrow   Amalia Guglielminetti (1891–1941)/Italy

I feel tomorrow's shadow, stuck,
waiting, by my pillow,
with Good and Bad held in its hands.

Is Bad kept hid in the left?
Is Good kept hid in the right?
Which will be offered me. Which?

And sleep comes, down waving ways,
and hums to me – *Don't worry... sleep now!*
and lays its finger softly on my eyes.

Sleep. Bitter hours may be fastened
in tomorrow's fist. Better not to worry.
Forget the shadow's silent spy that waits

to pounce, all ready, when you wake.

5

Death Poem   Hjálmar Jónsson (1796–1875)/Iceland

How stiff I find it now to write
and wag my trembled pen aright.
Alas, I barely sleep at night.
The dark admits of little light.
And I am cold, arthritic, bent and beat.

I stare into the darkness of defeat.
I hold my way along a dead-end street.
My grave gapes cold. I see my winding-sheet.
I cut my hope-shield runes to spite defeat –
read them who may, beyond my long, last fight.

*

Notes

1. Sleepless: new
2. I come from foggy, faroff lands: new
3. Lullaby: from 'The Song Atlas' (slightly revised)
4. Tomorrow: from '52 Euros' (slightly re-lined)
5. Death Poem: new

Letter from Wales

SAM ADAMS

As I have probably mentioned before, whenever I've felt sufficiently in funds I have bought antiquarian and private press books, persuading myself that, if the need ever arose, I could sell them again at a handsome profit. This is a spurious argument but I am always persuaded by it. Private press books are, or should be, objects of the printer's and illustrator's art, and the best are eminently readable into the bargain. A recent addition to my small collection is *The Autobiography of Edward Lord Herbert of Cherbury*, an impressively large Gregynog folio. Reading it and reading around it has been exhilarating.

The Herberts stem from William ap Thomas, a member of the Welsh gentry, subsequently knighted, who by marriage acquired wealth, prestige and eventually a grand property, Llansantfffraed Court, between Abergavenny and Raglan. His second wife was Gwladys Ddu, the daughter of Dafydd Gam, the Davy Gam of *Henry V*, and it is quite possible that as a young man he too fought at Agincourt. He died in 1445 and you will find him in full armour lying beside his wife on the impressive tomb they share in the Priory Church of St Mary, Abergavenny. The Herbert name was adopted when William ap Thomas, who had fought on the side of Edward IV in the Wars of the Roses, was granted the title Baron Herbert of Raglan. His son, also Sir William, dropped the Welsh patronymic. The Herberts were then firmly established as a prominent if not the pre-eminent mid-Wales family early in the sixteenth century and, in the usual way by marriage and astute purchase (and, doubtless, here and there sharp practice) extended ownership and influence over large tracts of Wales, north and south, even as far as Caerleon. Their copiously emblazoned family tree includes the poet George Herbert (1593–1633) and his older brother Edward (1583–1648), two of the ten children of Richard Herbert (d. 1596) and Margaret Newport (1565–1627). That the widowed Margaret, patron and friend of John Donne, who elegised her in 'The Autumnal', re-married a much younger John Danvers may suggest that a great deal of the physical liveliness and quick intelligence of her sons came from her. Another branch of the Herbert clan descended from William ap Thomas bears the 'incomparable pair of brethren' William Herbert (1580–1630) 3rd Earl of Pembroke, and Philip (1580–1630) Earl of Montgomery, to whom Shakespeare's First Folio is dedicated. The latter was known as 'the Welsh Lord' and (we are told in *The Dictionary of Welsh Biography*) was 'twitted with need for an interpreter'.

Edward is paradoxically described in the same source as 'a vain, sensitive man, a bold and profound thinker... a strange mixture of philosopher and buffoon'. He is the Renaissance figure reclining in a glade in reproductions of the exquisite full-length portrait miniature by Isaac Oliver that now resides in Powis Castle. Edward was born at his grandmother's house a few miles over the border at Eyton, Shropshire, but his home was Montgomery Castle, a link in the chain of mostly early thirteenth-century fortresses built to keep down the Welsh. By his own account he was so sickly as an infant and so slow to speak that it was feared he was deaf and he was left untutored in his early years. At seven he began making up for lost time. Aged nine he was taught Welsh, the everyday language of the host of peasants who scratched a living from the Herbert lands, and in due course he acquired Greek, Latin, French, Italian and Spanish. He was twelve when he was enrolled at University College, Oxford, but was shortly afterwards recalled home on the death of his father. For dynastic reasons, in 1598, Edward, now fifteen, was married to Mary, the twenty-one-year-old daughter of another branch of the Herbert family and, accompanied by his bride and his mother, returned to Oxford. In his memoir he disarmingly observes of this match that, 'having a due remedy for that lasciviousness to which youth is naturally inclined, I followed my book more close than ever'. After a decade of marital content, he fell into dispute with his wife regarding the inheritance of their children in the event of his death and her re-marriage. Because she refused to agree the guarantee he sought, he left her, pregnant, and departed for the continent.

Wherever he went his handsome looks and swashbuckling behaviour attracted attention. Visiting Paris in 1608, he was introduced to M. de Montmorency, the Constable of France, and was entertained by Marguerite de Valois and the Princess de Conti, impressing with his style and gallantry. In July 1610 he crossed the Channel again, on this occasion in the company of Lord Chandos and with serious purpose. In a fresh phase of the Eighty Years' War (1568–1648), an English expedition had been mounted under the command of Sir Edward Cecil to join Dutch, Brandenburg and Palatine forces besieging Juliers (Jülich), then occupied by the Habsburg Emperor Rudolf II. Herbert claimed to be among the first to enter the city. And when war flared there again in 1614 he returned as a volunteer in the army of the Prince of Orange. He had a hunger for war and adventure not easily satisfied and, if peace was unavoidable and no one available with whom he could pick a quarrel and fight a duel, a passion for learning. He studied antiquities in Rome and attended lectures at the university in Padua. Perhaps at last tiring of armed conflict, he leaned on his capacity for forging friendships with European nobility and sought the role of ambassador, eventually successfully. He opened negotiations for the marriage of Prince Charles and Princess Henrietta Maria, but there were other European alliances at stake and a falling out with King James led to his dismissal in 1624. Payment for his diplomatic services had been at best irregular and often entirely neglected: he left Paris deeply in debt. An Irish peerage was the kingly response and, after further petitioning, the gift of the manor of Ribbesford in Worcestershire. In May 1629 he was made Lord Herbert of Cherbury and in June 1637 became a member of the council of war. But his allegiance to Charles was not strong. He fended off invitations to join the king's forces and retired to his castle, where in due course he surrendered to troops of Sir Henry Middleton.

Before leaving Paris in 1609 he oversaw the printing of a philosophical work, *De Veritate, Prout Distinguitur a Revelatione, a Verisimili, a Possibili, et a Falso* ('On truth, in distinction from revelation, probability, possibility, and error'), which is recognised as the basis of Deism – belief in God as the Supreme Being that created the universe, but does not intervene in it. God's presence is revealed through Nature, and not in mystical revelation however mediated. (One suspects R.S. Thomas was Deist rather than orthodox Christian.) This does not imply an unshackled human free-for-all; Edward Herbert emphasised the roles of virtue and piety, and of remorse and repentance for sins. He found followers in Voltaire and Rousseau, and in Thomas Paine. It is unsurprising then that a fair number of America's Founding Fathers, including Benjamin Franklin, Thomas Jefferson and George Washington, might have thought of themselves as Deists.

Repair Work

MARIA STEPANOVA

In October 2023 Maria Stepanova won the Berman Literature Prize for *In Memory of Memory* (Fitzcarraldo Editions). This is her acceptance speech, translated from the Russian by Sasha Dugdale.

Dear Friends,
The book we are speaking of today was written only recently, and yet it was written in a different historical era – before the pandemic, when for a few years the whole world lived in a constant present tense: without the future, which had been put off indefinitely, and without the past, which seemed beyond reach. It was published before the beginning of a full-scale war of aggression in Europe, a war that was started and is still being waged by the country I was born in, and where I had spent my whole life. It is a war which has forever changed my sense of self and of my occupation. And that is why it is so hard for me to speak now. *In Memory of Memory* appeared in a different world and in some ways was written by a different person. The book was the product of a utopia that is still dear to me; I have always perceived Russia to be an integral part of a European cultural and historic space, a space which draws together thousands of individual fates into one, thousands of threads into a common weave. Now, when my compatriots insist that this communality does not exist and in fact never has, and the language I consider to be my native language is being used to justify violence and destruction, this vision seems a naive one.

The idea of communality, of one large conversation ranging across state borders and language barriers, has become problematic, and not just in Russia. Across the world right-wing parties and governments use similar arguments and methods – and their new form of common interest, based on fear and distrust towards all that is new or foreign, has a backward-looking, conservative quality. We are instructed to turn away from the future, with its frightening newness, and put our faith in political ideals based on the past. But not the real past – rather a fictional one, made to order and touched up and airbrushed to look more attractive. In Russia (but not just in Russia) special legislation has been passed to criminalise historical views that don't align with the officially-approved version: laws against the 'falsification of history' have made any discussion of state criminality a crime in itself. Historical knowledge and understanding based on facts and documented evidence have been replaced with an invented history. We are invited to learn this invention well, *memorise* it, and never deviate from its path. History is being squeezed out by memory, step by step, and sometimes we aren't even able to tell the difference between the two.

In the book we are speaking of today I wrote about all this, although it seemed to me back then that memory (or its dark, dangerous twin) had not yet flooded the known world:

> Memory is handed down, history is written down; memory is concerned with justice, history with preciseness; memory moralizes, history tallies up and corrects; memory is personal, history dreams of objectivity; memory is based not on knowledge, but on experience: compassion with, sympathy for a desperate pain demanding immediate involvement. At the same time the landscape of memory is strewn with projections, fantasies and misrepresentations – the ghosts of today, with their faces turned to the past.

Today these ghosts have swum to the surface; any version of the past and present has the potential to become a dogma if someone is willing to kill in its name. Russia's war against Ukraine is, amongst other things, a war of memory, an attempt to insist on one's own version of history with the aid of tanks and bombs and death. It is terrifying for me to consider what versions might come next.

All my life so far has been lived in a post-war world, a world which emerged following a catastrophe, the destruction of millions of lives in the name of a future that someone felt to be better, more perfect. War back then had particular defining features: it was spoken of in a way which left us as children in no doubt that we might well not have existed – that our whole existence was contingent on those who had died in a war thirty years before, and had died *that we might live*. As newspapers and books explained, they had sacrificed themselves so we could be born. This placed on us, the living, obligations of a particular kind, we were to live according to particular rules: to study well, behave ourselves, to be good children. It was as if our own lives didn't entirely belong to us – we had to earn the posthumous approval of dead strangers. The role our own country played in the dividing up of Poland, in occupying other territories and in mass killings, was not part of the public understanding, and so it was easy and natural to see ourselves as representatives of the force of good.

Another catastrophe, the destruction of the old world as it was at the turn of the century, was spoken of less, and in every family it was spoken of in a different way, because it had no limits and no common characteristics. It was a kind of secret which needed to be hidden from others, and those who knew it (and those with whom one could share it) were filled with alternating feelings of pride and shame when they found out. Scratch at the glossy daytime sheen of any family, including your own, and a *weak point* will soon be found – something that must never be discussed at school, and at home was only communicated in strained and hushed voices, so you intuitively knew it was a serious matter. It took years to begin to speak openly, and years more to learn how to listen and distinguish between the stories of neighbours or school friends. It became suddenly clear that a deep abyss of misfortune was secreted at the heart of every family, not just ours – every family had their own, quite unlike anyone else's.

In our home, a secular Jewish household, in which the old religion had been replaced by the (still fairly ancient) cult of learning and culture, the black hole that one could never quite suppress or understand – and in understanding it, hold it at bay – was the catastrophe of European Jewry and what had led to it over the decades, from blood libels to pogroms. This was talked about endlessly, unsparingly, in all its terrible detail. But I needed to grow up before realising that the realm of the unspoken lay alongside what could be spoken of: here unyielding silence reigned to the end, and not all the forbidden subjects were to do with being Jewish. The history of my family was filled with torn threads, fates which I will probably never find out, and can only guess at, based on what happened in Odessa in 1919 during the Red Terror, or in 1941 when Hitler's army took the city, or in Rzhev in 1942 when all the inhabitants of the Jewish ghetto were murdered, or in Kherson at the beginning of the 1920s when each side took it in turns to rule the town, each worse than the last. The frankness with which my mother told me about the Holocaust had a shadowy reverse side: from her I heard only about those who survived. We were the ones who had survived. As Primo Levi said: the worst survived, the best perished.

We, then, were the *worst* among the *just-as-bad*, and telling us apart from the next person in the tram carriage or in the doctor's waiting room was only possible by the particular nature of our phantom pain. Around me in the dusty atmosphere of the late USSR were the children and grandchildren of those who hadn't been able to save themselves: peasants (repressed and exiled, starved, shot during grain requisitioning), labourers (sent to camps, shot), those 'people of the past' as they were termed: merchants, petty bureaucrats, priests, the gentry, who had hidden themselves in nooks and priest-holes for decades and were doomed to gradual destruction. And then there were the descendants of those who had carried out the executions: countless secret policemen and Red Army soldiers who were prepared to kill in order to build a new world in which the previously insignificant could reign supreme. And yet even for them things almost always ended badly, as they had done for everyone else. They in turn became 'enemies of the people' without even knowing how, and lay themselves down in the pits of executed bodies alongside the rest.

In this way everyone became a victim, apart from those who survived. All were made equal: not in a good way, but by the common grave, the common fate. Even the idea of picking through the headstones, trying to decide who was good and who less so, seemed somehow clumsy. All this was bewildering – from afar it seemed to us that in postwar Europe there were only three simple categories to remember: victims, murderers and witnesses, and it was impossible to confuse them. Whereas every second one of us had contrived to alternate between the categories, and had settled in the end on the third: the executioner's pit. But execution without trial or due process, extrajudicial death, seemed in some way to cancel out what had come before – so the millions of dead were just clotted together as one mass of great tragedy, without any explanation ('that's what it was like' shrugged our elders) or way of differentiating. Revolution, civil war, collectivisation, the Terror, the Second World War, another period of State Terror – there is not a single family who emerged intact from this machine of death. And as there could be no retribution, nor even consolation or explanation for these deaths, all that was left to us, born a few decades later, was to study well, behave ourselves, be good children – and to carry within, like the yolk of an egg, the long memory of what can never be set right; and self-pity, because after all anything could happen to you, too.

Fear and self-pity: everything that is needed to see in oneself not an actor or subject of history, but merely its raw material. You could simply ignore your own part in this whirlpool of violence or consider yourself as having been coerced into action: not the leg kicking the ball, but the ball itself, that flies up, striking walls and human bodies. The Soviet utopia allowed the possibility of considering yourself guilt-free – or at least only partially guilty, a small screw in a huge mechanism that kept going whether you liked it or not. Inside this killing machine personal responsibility was easy to evade, either with the mimicry that was essential to survival ('I did what everyone did'), or by adopting moral standards for exceptional circumstances ('those were just the times we lived in'). My generation inherited not just horror at the twentieth century and its wholesale killing, but also the feeling that our family members had suffered greatly, and in a way beyond comprehension or comparison. We were the survivors and we were grateful to our close family that they had managed not to die.

This suffering, the narrow corridor of its solipsism, permits no view of the overall picture, nor of one's place in it, nor what went on beyond the margins of the Soviet experiment – giving the illusion of a particular kind of innocence. It was something like a letter of safe passage. Millions of people felt themselves to be victims of circumstance or the results of circumstance – but never the circumstances themselves, nor the force to change them.

I say 'we', where two years ago I would have insisted on 'I', speaking from my personal experience; considering it unique, as any individual experience is. Saying 'we' now is not an attempt to slough off my responsibilities, to lay them on the collective 'shoulder' (that is, on no one's shoulder), but my sense that a private existence, when understood as a conscious choice, is also the evasion of a problem that must be resolved. In what we call 'troubled societies'* the feeling that one is not to blame, a sense of one's apartness, difference or non-participation, is essential in order to survive and stay sane. But on the other hand, these singular private existences, all believing themselves to be uninvolved and free from the general stain, when taken together, give birth to a society in which every person sees themselves as a heroic loner, outside the structures of power and the exchange of violence, and the pronoun 'we' is seen as an attack on personal boundaries. As a result we lose the ability to resist, as well as the ability to discern and differentiate. Events that are determined by class, gender, cultural structures, are easier to behold when one floats above them like a balloon with no one to pull on its string. This distancing effect allows strange things to happen: a person can work for a propaganda channel or shoot at other men exactly like himself, believing at the same time that these actions have no relation to his real and authentic self, and this self remains aloof and apart, a bystander. 'I did my work', 'I followed orders', 'I didn't know anything', 'I believed what the papers wrote'. It is always others who are guilty, and we direct our righteous anger at them in order to hide from ourselves the knowledge of our own similar choices. Living in a particular society, and yet believing oneself free of its imprint, is one of the features which has made it possible for Russia to become what it is today. The fact that our historical passivity has its reasons, a succession of choices and refusals to choose, the inability to become what one might provisionally call 'a political nation', does not remove my responsibility for not being part of a collective and functioning 'we'.

I used to think of myself as part of a different community, one that was not defined by historical experience or state boundaries, and my work as part of this community also causes me pain in retrospect, and forces me to ask questions of myself. Towards the end of the sixties, in Europe and beyond, a new and powerful intellectual movement arose over the rubble of the old world: names, stories, caesurae, homes left empty, destroyed cities and villages, children left without even a memory of their parents. This movement was driven by the sense that there was no task more important than gathering up the pieces and recreating, remembering, committing to memory everything that could be saved. It had a spontaneous, almost elemental quality; to begin with it was barely conscious of itself and it had no attachment to a language or nation. But in the thirty or forty years that followed, it created what was in effect a new cultural movement (even the noted German *Erinnerungskultur* is only one of its manifestations), going well beyond the limits of museums, publishing programmes and academic discourse. Its main feature is a deep attention to and interest in any form of the past, down to every single tiny shard of porcelain or faded black-and-white photograph.

We live in a world where the past (a past the twentieth century wanted to tear itself away from) has entirely filled the public imagination, occupying the space of both present and future. Everything that relates to the past has acquired a special and disproportionately inflated value. Bookshelves groan under the weight of documentary novels bringing forgotten names and undervalued figures back into the light; the less-known the person, the more excitement there is in telling her tale. The price of objects from the past rises fast – now no one throws out grandad's sticks of furniture, they take them to antique shops, where the concept of 'vintage' makes anything too young to be antique commercially viable. The volume of second-hand clothing sold goes up from year to year. Advertising and postcards draw on images from the twenties, thirties and fifties and the fashion industry does the same; for a few decades now it has been almost entirely devoted to referencing and reworking what was invented many years before. The past has long ago outgrown the period when it was simply the object of nostalgic curiosity, and it has become a powerful economic factor affecting our daily life in dozens of imperceptible ways. The political consequences are by now impossible to escape: controlling the past, attempting to harness it, monopolise it, rewrite it according to taste, have all become part of electoral and legislative processes in many countries in Europe and beyond. For those who can't bear the thought of inevitable change or the promised new, the past is a paradise lost (one which never existed, and is therefore especially attractive), and also a weapon to use against the future.

But it doesn't stop there. Right in front of us a sort of thinking which belongs entirely in the past has returned to the world's discourse. This way of thinking had been considered archaic, out-of-date, gone forever – but with each passing year its presence is more evident. Once again the comparative qualities of different ethnicities are discussed (and which nations are inferior, non-existent, or just plain *bad*), blood and soil, the right of the strongest, the health of the nation. We are moving backwards into the twentieth century at the same speed we once ran from it. Another reason why Russian aggression against Ukraine is horrific is that it is a twentieth-century war, both in the means of warfare, and the ideas behind it.

We didn't expect this. I didn't think it would come. Before our eyes the era of memory, individual and collective, darkens at its heart. The attempt to preserve fragments of the lost world, perhaps even to collect them into a partial but coherent picture, seems a helpless one alongside the state projects with the single goal of selling the electorate a false memory of the past, with even the traces of recent catastrophe erased, glorified, made compatible with life. As sometimes happens with ideas that are at their outset driven by an ethical imperative,

* Maria uses these English words in her original

a pure and passionate desire to see justice done, and are suddenly more successful than could have been hoped to be, memorialising has become its opposite in today's reality: a deliberately cynical effort to create oblivion. What started as a movement to unite people and rid ourselves of generational and cultural stereotypes in the service of a single moral endeavour has begun to sink into a nostalgia of a completely different and terrifying nature.

I was and remain a part of this unnamed and unbounded movement. From my very childhood and long before I began writing what would become *In Memory of Memory* I was captivated by the past – just as Marianne Hirsch writes in her book on 'Postmemory', it was infinitely more interesting than my own utterly ordinary life. My texts, from poems to essays, are, above all else, connective tissue joining fragments of the lost, the words of others, or what is left of them. In this regard my work is like the darning of socks or the mending of clothes, that historically female occupation, undemanding but essential in the past before overproduction led us to unlearn the skill of lengthening the life of objects that had served their owners rightfully and faithfully. It is a peace-filled craft that fixes and strengthens, and I feel sad when I think of memory today and how it has forgotten itself and become an instrument of violence and separatism, a dead tongue, a bringer of death. I never wanted that, we (this time the hardly-bounded, impossible-to-describe 'we' of people who have worked for years on the restoration of the past and of memory) never wanted that.

It reminds me in some ways of the language I write and think in, the language I am talking to you in: Russian. For many people it is now the symbol and instrument of violence and oppression. The language does not bear responsibility for what is happening; unlike us it makes no decisions and choices. Like memory, language depends entirely on us, it changes with us, and becomes the first victim of our desperation and our unwillingness to act. Memory and language have only us to place their hope in, and if we leave them to the whims of fate, or the mercy of those who would attempt to make monsters of them, then the burden of our guilt only grows heavier. Mutilated, damaged, unrecognisable, but still alive, language and memory could still be recovered and returned – and my job is to help in this.

Tikkun olam, an ancient concept from the realm of Jewish mysticism, is derived from the knowledge that the world we live in is damaged and nearly irreparably broken, and that the job of the living is the work of reconstruction, the repair work: if you see a hole then darn it as best you can. There is nothing grandiose about this, it has nothing in common with the terrifying collective projects of the twentieth century which aimed to create a new world, a new man, and in doing so nearly destroyed humanity, and the world. Once it seemed as if memory was a talisman, a security against events repeating themselves: *never again*. Today it too is in need of repair work.

The concept of *tikkun olam* seems incredibly, painfully relevant, as actual as it once seemed to Gershom Scholem, when he wrote that the doctrine 'raised every Jew to the rank of a protagonist in the great process of restitution'. Today I too subscribe to these very words, although perhaps I would replace 'every Jew' with 'every person'. That would be more precise, especially now, when the life-tissue is in shreds, and not only in Europe but throughout the known world. Every one of us, and I think of myself first of all, needs to take up needle and thread and begin the repair work.

Some Uncollected Poems

JAMES K. BAXTER

Selected by Roger Hickin

James K. Baxter wrote in the introduction to his selected poems, *The Rock Woman* (1969), of 'an obsessive industry that led [him] as often as not into the cactus'. The poems that follow are from *A Branch Torn Down*, a forthcoming selection – the fourth such – of work unpublished and uncollected in Baxter's lifetime, work that doesn't always avoid the cactus, but does attest to the deep involvement in the human condition of New Zealand's most talented, prolific and controversial poet, 'a passionate, complex and haunted man' who was also, in John Weir's view, 'one of the great English-language poets of the twentieth century'.

A Portrait of a Fellow-Alcoholic

My cobber has the shakes. The whitish-red
Eyes glitter in the punchbag of his head –
'That bugger Reilly never had the right
To bash me when I bent under the bed

To get my fiddle...' The ice-black urinal
In which he lay till dawn, more dead than tight,
Has fouled his jersey. In the trim lounge bar
I shout him three good whiskies for the trip

To the casualty ward – 'On Guy Fawkes night
I pulled the American Consul from his car
To get five shillings for another jar;
They've got no brains at all,

The bloody cops. I've given them the slip
Since Saturday...' Mother, have mercy on
Two idiot burnt brothers walking by
That cindered Phlegethon

Whose waves of fire and blackness I
Know better than the Mass. At the hospital
We sit for two hours on the varnished bench
Waiting for the quack. The nurse draws back

With a screwed mouth from the white spirit stench.
The ants begin to bite; the steel whips crack.
Tonight in 1A, scrubbed and dried,
He'll suck a sponge dipped in formaldehyde.
(1962)

Regret at Being a Pakeha

Sea-egg, puha, pork and kumara,
Eaten among friends,
A bridge between the living and the dead:

These things should be enough.

A man and his shovel digging a drain,
Talk of women in the sun,
The touch of bodies in consolation:

These things should be enough.

Old wounds forgiven, happiness remembered,
Song at the altar of reconciling
And silence when the branch is bare:

Were it not that we carry as miners do
Our hard identity, a crust of dust,
A tombstone always in the living lungs.
(1963)

Song of the Mercy of Saint Anne

(after Tristan Corbière)

Old woman with breasts of black rimu
Carved by the chisel, hear me!
Under the veined wood your heart is alive,
The heart of a pakeha Maori.

Mother, we have seen your face
When the creeks are in flood,
Among the green fern your tears of mercy,
And from the dry earth tears of blood!

If an altar stands close like a sore thumb
How shall your antique breast
Grow plump to feed the mouth of Mary
Whose virginity folded the son to rest

Like the deep sea? Grant then,
Saint Anne, cradle and ark
For the unborn light, and for the poor a blanket
To keep them alive in the dark –

God's grandmother, you who knitted
A suit for the Boy at Bethlehem,
And sewed in trouble the heavy stitch
Of the shroud at Jerusalem!

You whose wrinkles are gouged crosses,
Whose hair is whiter than thread,
Bare rock of silence, nurse of the newly born
And layer-out of the dead!

Ark of Joachim! Shall we burn
Like rats in a farmer's pit
Where dead sheep, maggots, kerosene,
Blaze, and the fire eats into the fat?

A cloud-burst, Lady, from your eyes,
When God is occupied, would put
Hell out of action – Only make for me
A bed in the shearers' hut;

Nothing elaborate. Remember, though,
The drunk with a cramp in his legs
Under the black fires – lead him
Gently between the cops and the kegs

To a bright room. And the young wife like a heifer
Panicking as her pains begin,
Grip her hand, wise woman, and teach her
What it is to give birth to a man.

The old ones, Lady, with brittle bones,
Who think of what is gone, and get no ease,
Catch them up at midnight suddenly
To the green Sabbath of God's peace.

For those who die in wards when the lights are grey
Sweating and fighting for breath,
Hold up the cross and shove Hell's pack away,
Lady of holy death!

Dragon who guarded the Virgin, keep good watch
On the kids who swing on ropes by the river;
And when they are sick, give each one in a dream
A drink of soda water.

Don't forget the girl with the wandering man
Sitting dolled-up in front of the TV set
Like a watch with a broken spring – turn, if you can,
The plastic heart back into a heart of flesh

And the man who has plodded so far on his own feet
That leather, cloth and flesh are gone,
Give him (I beg you) nothing else to eat
But the berries of the snow, a soldier's ration.

The lass in a well-off family's oubliette,
Where the shrunk heads glare to break her spirit,
Before they trim her guts with the curette
Give her the teeth and the claws of a ferret!

And the boy dressed like a girl who has dreamt he is Satan
Sleepwalking by the ships,
Tell him his nature is Joseph's coat of blood
And say goodnight to him from the waves' lips.

For such things, Mother, I will kneel to you
And burn a candle
For half a crown (the cost of a drink or two)
This Friday in your Daughter's chapel.
(1964)

A Christmas Sadness

I think of an old man gutted by
The four devils of the West,
Warm heart, home trouble, dead work, abstract thought,
Climbing in the season's heavy breast
A bush track to the sky,

To find, cold and late, at the scrub farm
From the door of a dark whare a light,
And a Maori girl with a child on her arm,
Black haired, in a blue dress, whose voice
Like water under fern flows out –

'Come in, Jack, and rest.'

But he looks with pale, old eyes
At the sea that swallows down a meteorite,
At lawyer bushes, graveyard earth,
And the track that is itself the night.
(1964)
[whare: house]

Virtue and Death

I notice how my friend the drunken tobacconist
Who lies with the cramps and the shits on a bumpy
  mattress
At the back of his shop, talks of his dead mad wife
As 'a real lady' – virtue, death,

Are the same words to him – I also,
These cloud-dark afternoons with work to do,
Dawdle in the kitchen, read old letters,
And see for a minute in my mind's eye

An invalid child in a bed like a snow-covered paddock
Doing nobody any harm –
Quiet as a doorknob, he waits
For his Mum to bring him a drink, for the sun to rise;

The bad ones are down at the river, smoking and fighting;
He hears them shout like rowdy daylight ghosts
From half way down the road – he waits, I wait,
To live, to die, for some great horn

To blow and split the sky – virtue, death,
Too much connected, somehow –
Gentlemen, ladies, I ask you to examine
My halo of bright maggots!
(1967)

The Cattle Shed

(for Janet Frame)

Do you remember that afternoon in winter
When we left the town of bones behind us, and
  walked on
Up the Leith Valley road? All of us
Were wet as shags! Your coat and hair were wet.
Branches unloaded rain on us. The creek
Was talking all along the gully
About whatever suits a water spirit,

And we climbed further up to a cattle shed,
Crossing the soaking clumps of cocksfoot grass
With wet shoes. We sat down
Among the rusted harnesses,
And ate our bread and sausage,

And you spoke of Andorra – how those churches
Are built like barns out of the valley rock –
Being ourselves in such a place; as if, Janet,
To have been born were enough, as I incline
To think it is. You and Jacquie
Made water on the dung-black floor

Before we left. I remember it as a barn
Made out of rock; a womb; a stopping-place.
(1966)

Spring Sonnets 1968

1
The girl with the broad brass belt and the yellow matador
Pants that leave her waist naked is going

Down the stairs in front of me. This travelling body
Obstructs my view of nature. If the cold sharp

Spring wind blows down from the snow on Mount Cargill
It whets in me the edge of self; I'd like to

Undress the goddess with an old man's frenzy
And die. Instead I natter about Shaw and Pinter

To Patric Carey. Drink one cup. Ignore her.
Aquinas, Aquinas, you can shove the Summa

Up your holy rectum! I want to be a singing
Jellyfish without a philosophy

Able to feed without remorse on those
Magnificent sullen lips and demon-yoking thighs.

2
At the top of the steps that lead to Haddon Place
Somebody has lit a fire of grass and branches

Whose smoke pleases me; and just above it
A fat Samoan child in a tartan shirt is playing

On the veranda slats. If the fire should grow
Suddenly larger, consuming first the house

With its five rooms, its TV set,
And the print of the Queen above the mantelpiece,

A royal pudding on horseback; then (I'll not disguise it)
Backyard by backyard the whole bog-built town –

The child might laugh, clapping his hands and shouting
At the fiery convolvulus. But this won't happen.

We die where we are born. The flames are all
Purely internal, eating the vein, the brain, the groin.

3
It is time to repent, time to kneel and say
A mouthful of Hail Marys in front of

The little Virgin the Bishop brought back from Spain
Paying no duty. She does not have to pour

A bucket on my head. This old incendiarist
Has lost his matches. Let us begin – 'Mother,

'It was a black birth when I came
Howling into the world. The green sprig

'Your Son planted has grown crookeder
With each blind season. I don't expect

'Miracles or another mountain to hide in
From the man-killing Dove. I bow the head.

'Grant what is. Give me rocks to eat.
I prefer always to be treated as a man.'
(1968)

Junkie House

The cold is freezing my toe joints
At 2 a.m. in this small room

In Grafton – my bed is low down on the floor
And the fleas boil out of the thin mattress

As soon as I lie down – in this old junkie house
Many things are at sixes and sevens

But the long yellow candle in front of the statue
Of Our Lady Help of Junkies will go on burning

For another four hours – its light on the bare walls
Shows that to believe is to have nothing

And to walk in the dark – to walk on the dark waves
Of each hour, sister, knowing that to be is the miracle,

And the great sun who is the brother of Christ
Will rise again and cradle us in his hands.
(1969)

Holy Sonnets

1
At noonday I sit on the communal dyke
And hear the bell ring for the Angelus –

'The Word was made Flesh' – the wasps come here in droves,
Partly because it is the season of fruit

When apples and wild blackberry
Are ready for eating, and partly

Because they can catch blowflies
Round this cavern where we drop our shit

Fifteen feet. Lord, you made the green pungas
That roar in the wind on the hill ridges

Between us and the sky, and for us the pain
Of incompleteness, like the bruised aching gut

Of an old woman who has to watch
Her children's children play their rowdy games and die.

2
They have cleared the ground very nicely round the house;
What we walk on is thistles and the hacked off vines

Of blackberry. This hot day I go browsing
Like a goat on the ripening berries

Till my stomach is full of the watery pulp,
But at the broken house among the brambles

I go in the door, take off my shirt and jersey,
Hang them on two rusty nails on the wall,

And begin the old game of flogging my back
With the buckle of my belt – not too hard, not too lightly –

Thirty-nine strokes, the measure of Saint Paul, –
The cicadas chirrup on the grey-brown heads of cocksfoot,

The world won't change. Why do I keep on asking
Our Christ for the impossible? We were meant to blaze like the sun.

3
Lord, the food bill is one-sixty dollars;
I have ninety in the bank, –

If you want us to live on air and water cress
That's your business. Father, I can't find you;

I think the great bogs are bringing me down,
My throat is filling with mud. Yesterday

On the track between the church and the wharepuni
I looked for you and couldn't find you.

What is the point of quarrelling? Why should I want more
Than a hole in the ground to hide in

And boards to keep my body from the wet?
I am sin. There's nothing new in that.

Father, all I want is for you to turn me
Inside out like a stranded octopus.
(1972)

[Now in the darkness of the moon]

Now in the darkness of the moon
The wind blows this way from the graveyard,

And my heart is failing – so long a journey
I have to undertake, setting aside

The lips and the hands of women
That guarded and imprisoned me

Since the day that I was born. It may be, my friend,
After the ninth or the twenty-seventh day

The wind that carries dust will bring the smell
Of flowers growing. To be no longer man

Is what I fear, bending my head
In the darkness of this cave. The face I see

Is not the face of love but the face of night.
I am drinking the waters of the underworld.
(1972)

Last Exit for the Revolution

ROD MENGHAM

In May of 2023 I looked inside the psyche of the GDR and saw its dying visions. The architectural cranium where this mirage lingers is a building the size of a power station, looming over the hamlet of Bad Frankenhausen in the state of Thuringia. Its location is not easy to access, or even find. The last stage of a thirty-six-hour journey from Harwich involves a very slow train from Erfurt to Heldrungen – where there is a halt, rather than a station – and then a bus ride (no. 491) that delivers small children to school and pensioners to the local GP. The terminus at Bad Frankenhausen is a lorry park on the last area of level ground before the southern slopes of the Kyffhäuser range lead up to the Schlachtberg, which is where the most quixotic art project ever conceived in Eastern Europe was finally installed in 1989, a mere eight weeks before the fall of the Berlin Wall.

I was seconded for this mission by Leo Mellor: Cambridge fixer, envoy of Welsh poetry – and psychopomp for the German weird. Leo had prepared a faultless itinerary, but there was no preparing for the off-piste, the unmapped yet very stubborn obstacles to any traveller in the communist afterlife.

The small town's centre of gravity was downhill, but we needed to go up. We found the only cobbled street willing to oblige, and started to climb, alongside the most crooked church spire that either of us had ever seen (although it was only the second most crooked in Germany, we later learned). Very soon the street just gave up, ended. Never mind: there were paths – several paths in fact – willing to take over. They wound through the densely planted trees with just enough emphasis to convey a sense of purpose, but they hadn't signed a contract to properly finish the job, and didn't. We paused: in the middle of a dark wood the right way was lost, but faith would show us the way – not Dante's faith, but the faith of Werner Tübke, employed by the Central Committee of the Socialist Unity Party of Germany to plan and execute a monumental commemoration of the Peasants' Rebellion of the 1520s, led by the proto-communist priest Thomas Müntzer. The final, desperate battle had taken place on top of the hill we were climbing, and Tübke's panoramic painting was intended as the screen on which it could be projected all over again.

When we emerged from the trees, we found ourselves in an empty car park connected to a concrete path that led out of sight but up the hill. The borders of this path were carefully curated, with shrubs and saplings, which gave our vagaries an instant upgrade – we were now clearly on the sanctioned approach. The path was narrow, but with a gradient so slight, it turned our experimental amble into a stately progress. And then we saw it – an enormous barrel-shaped building with all the aesthetic properties of a nuclear facility: half missile silo, half cathedral, a suitable container for the aesthetic ideology of the future. And it had a swimming pool. The swimming pool seemed like a diversionary tactic – who would think of taking their swimming costume to visit the fourth dimension of art? There must be an ulterior motive: or perhaps it was a way of saying, welcome to the world of ulterior motives.

The swimming pool was an outdoor antechamber to the entrance hall: a wide plate-glass assembly point, with a small bookshop plus ticket office on the right, and a café counter on the left. We were cheered by the sight of the latter – without having consciously suppressed all appetite, we both now felt a pressing need for Küche before Kultur. But there was a hitch: the cook had not turned up for work. I felt the passage of time between 1989 and 2023 collapse in an instant, remembering many occasions during the 1980s when East German or Polish restaurants could offer only one waiter, only one of the dishes on the menu, and only one kind of alcohol. Leo and I compromised by swigging a couple of poolside beers, and reflecting on the matter of fact way in which the barmaid had cancelled lunch. 'Clearly no room for self-doubt at this inn' Leo declared.

We drank up and proceeded to the ticket booth, where we were re-directed to the cloakroom, with earnest instructions to deposit pretty much everything except our own selves in the hands of the receiving committee. Suitably disarmed, we returned to the ticket-selling committee, which pressed us to rent helmets – the sort telling you that what you are looking at is not what you think but what the helmet thinks. We declined, to the evident distress of the old lags. That they were old lags, every last one of them, we had little doubt. They were of an age. They held themselves upright in their uniforms. They took pride in their work, and the institution they served. They had done the State some service. But which State? That was the question. When they spoke, it was as if they were wearing a helmet; but a different kind of helmet, the sort that gets implanted.

With shows of great courtesy and conciliation on both sides, we were eventually released, to fend for ourselves in the unending class battle of Tübke's panorama. The viewing chamber was hushed and darkened, with the only available light suffusing the walls to which the panorama had been attached. Once our eyes had got used to the murk, we could make out a fair number of viewers peering up from their stations on a series of stuffed fabric columns like a circle of mushrooms in the middle of the room. The viewers, nearly all of a certain age, shared an attitude that might have been a kind of expectant reverence, as if they were taking part in a political history séance. They were all apparently in a state of disbelief at Tübke's spectacle of belief – of a creed doomed in the 1520s, but which had seemed enduring, just, in the 1980s.

It is fair to say that Tübke was not a great artist, but he was an expert painter whose sensibility was steeped in the conventions of Renaissance and Mannerist art. Half the content of the panorama consists of realistic depictions of episodes in the conflict between the army of the peasants and the mercenary forces employed by the nobles. The other half floats in an allegorical or symbolic realm, although its agents and patients occupy the same landscape as the historical figures. The panorama does what it says on the tin, extending all the way round the interior of the viewing hall. But at what feels like the conceptual centre of the painting there is a group portrait of pioneers of the Northern Renaissance, including Albrecht Dürer, Martin Luther, Lucas Cranach the Elder, Philipp Melanchthon, Erasmus of Rotterdam, Nicholas Copernicus, Paracelsus and Johannes Gutenberg. They are grouped symbolically around the 'Wellspring of Life', which is artificially hedged off from the main battlefield. Tübke is aligning the confrontation of peasants and mercenaries in 1525 with a broader historical shift in which independent scientific research is challenging traditional concepts of social order and authority. The peasants lose the battle but embody a movement towards the radical revaluation of the relations of power, allegiance and entitlement.

Remember that Tübke's conceptual scheme has to line up with the programmatic ambitions of state socialism – which it does – but is also full of cracks. And out of these cracks spring a number of weird distractions from the main plan: a large translucent blue fish floats through a snowbound landscape past a half-ruined Tower of Babel, where it releases a second deluge in the form of a liquid funnel that generates new life; meanwhile, a vividly blue pool of liquid or gas surrounds a raging red inferno in the centre of which a boiling cauldron contains a blackened human head screaming in pain (the pool is surrounded by nobles and church dignitaries understandably puzzled by this spectacle); in the distance, there is a crucifixion scene contained within a transparent globe with a large rip in one side – and in front of this a menacing blue angel waves a palm branch at a recoiling man who holds his head in his hands as if unable to process what is happening. There are many such combinations of strong imagery and suspended meaning. Tübke is enumerating all the faultlines in early sixteenth-century culture that required dialectical thinking to make them amenable to human, as opposed to supernatural, intervention.

The tension arising from the contrast between everyday appearances and the outlandish extravagance of the late medieval imagination is managed artistically by Tübke's stylistic hesitation between the kind of physical realism to be found in Breughel's peopled landscapes and the brand of lurid metaphysical fantasies we associate with Hieronymus Bosch. The panorama is so enormous and so evenly attentive to local detail, it is all but impossible for the viewer to stabilise this relationship. If the ultimate objective of the artwork is a political critique of conditions demanding revolutionary change, its ultimate effect is to overwhelm and bewilder the viewer with the volume and variety of its distractions.

There are key individuals included in the overall melee, although they are as good as lost in the general confusion. Almost half the painted surface is taken up by the chaotic fighting of 15 May 1525. Tübke has fixed upon a moment when the tide is on the verge of turning in favour of the status quo. When you can find it, you can see that the focus is on the exhausted and downcast figure of Müntzer, whose face is drained of colour. The banner of the peasants in his left hand is already trailing on the ground. The whole of history is meant to pivot around this moment: a tactical defeat that nonetheless inspires a strategic plan, to be completed by future generations. The panorama executes a loop in space, and projects a vision of time as a closed system of permanent revolution. As a record of the Peasants' Revolt, it honours their sacrifice; as a blueprint for history, it accounts for every future success and failure as part of the revolutionary pattern. This is why it had to be a panorama. And it is also why the panorama had to be here, on the actual battlefield.

As we exited, blinking, from the viewing chamber, the attendants glanced in our direction. Had we seen what we were supposed to see? Were we initiates? We hadn't been told what to think, but were we thinking it anyway? We were actually thinking about lunch, if the truth be told. But not only lunch. We got outside, into the chilly air under those grey skies. But before heading off downhill, we found ourselves hanging around on the Schlachtberg, behind the panorama, musing on the ploughed-over fields where the battle was lost and won. They were obviously very productive fields, well fertilised: there was growth springing up everywhere. Lots of dead peasants had seen to that. Apart from a few distant birds, it was very quiet. The place seemed to elicit silence, and to expect a certain kind of attention. I don't think we knew how to respond to that, I know I didn't. So we turned round and headed back in the general direction of town. And very quickly we hit upon a dead straight path, going all the way downhill. There were several intersections, each with lateral dead straight paths to left and right, and all with invisible destinations. It was as if the paths were all opening up just for us and then closing again behind us.

It seems that no paths lead directly to the memory-sites of the GDR, yet all paths lead directly away from them.

The Citadel of the Mind

STAV POLEG

First you were an idea, a blue satellite
orbiting a distant, dark

moon. Then you were a feather, the light
distance it takes for beauty

to form into something like finding
the ground. It didn't happen

without warning, the morning
glowed like a feverish neon sign – an indication

of clemency – I thought, the sky
turned sapphire and dark like new foreign

fire – a transposition
from fear to loss – how wrong

I was. How wrong
was the weather, raining and raining

without pause. I've always thought
there was one primary source –

not light or fire but the small
movement from sound

into a word. The leaping fish
was glowing from blue to bright turquoise

when moving upstream
or was it a song I was trying

to catch – a foreign soundscape
floating above the wide-open highway

when heading back home? First
you were an idea. Then, an idea

with wings – something like flying
or shifting the weight between travel

and dream. Today, I'm reading
that *The Vita Nova tells of dream visions*

and feverish hallucinations. It's late
afternoon, the shortest

day of the year. There are so many ways
to lock oneself out of a castle, out of a word

that threatens to destabilise
a sentence, a faraway kingdom, the heart

of a scene. Love
and the trembling of light when it reaches

the water. Love like a highway – a misapprehension
of speed. First you were stretching

your arms, testing the wingspan of grief –
it was not theoretical – you've known

for too long how it feels. Knowledge
and grief – the strange forces

of water when they reach a new land –
no – it's not that. Knowledge

and grief – a theatre scene carrying
the weight of an unpronounced

word – no, not *quite* what I mean. First
you turned loss into a symbol, a primary

myth. Then you found dreaming – the sounds
taking flight in a faraway

street. That you carried a sign like a country –
that you weren't able to let go –

was that grief? The empiricist
insists on realism, dreams

may come later, dreams are the function
of a visual mind. Dreams are echoes

and interpretations. There's order, sure –
there's order even in chaos

theory – patterns, equations, the long
calculations of matter as time. The historian

considers primary sources as if they were numbers
not words. The poet is a pragmatist – making

something out of the strange promise
of nothing – words

are important but not *that*
important. First you were an idea, then

a dark river, an arrow, a field fractured
with lights. The philosopher seeks

the truth. Truth, the poet thinks, how unusual
and noble, how responsible

and full of trust. The poet is a pragmatist –
she prefers to play. Play, like sleep or love

is the most serious thing – the poet
claims. Sure – the physicist

says before heading towards the river
that cuts through opposite

notions of time – whatever you say.
In the *Convivio*, in the battle of knowledge

versus love – Lady Philosophy
wins, hands down. But Dante tells us

that Beatrice is still there, still walking
around, still *holding the citadel of my mind* –

the citadel of the mind –
like a chamber of flashing blue light –

is struck with new fire, lightning, the fierce
temper of rain. Time

has passed but the mind
does not do time. The mind refuses

time as a gift made of distance
and light. The physicist understands

time in relation to space
and gravity – time is the fourth dimension

in a physical non-metaphorical
sense: there is no such thing as Space

but Space-Time. The heart, the heart
is constructed of four chambers, the poet

tries. The poet studies time like a theatre
scene – the fourth wall

like a curtain of time between language
and play. On the stage, time

can be anything – a theatre
prop: an hourglass full of running blue

sand. The actor takes the small
hourglass before tossing it towards the ceiling

again and again. Time, like something
falling, time like a dark implication, a realization

of heat. The actor picks up
the broken, uneven

fragments of glass from the sand-covered
floor. The poet goes out of the theatre, takes

the first bus and starts running, running
in words. Reading physics is like drinking

ten cups of espresso in one
hour – the poet contemplates – my mind

is high on physics – my heart
is flying on so much caffeine. Time –

like a want or a miscalculation –
is that it? In the *Convivio*, letting

Beatrice go is turning her into a leading
idea – the sketch of a castle

before building a castle. Does it work? Well,
in the *Purgatorio*, Beatrice will come back

less as an idea, more as an undefeatable
force. First you were a satellite, then

a dark forest, a fortress of words. You turned love
into knowledge, darkness into a wrestling

ring – the audacity of language
when it gathers more speed. Yes, I know –

I must accept – not everything
is about loss. Not all philosophy

was forced to be written out of exile, the deep
soundscape or grief. Not every word

was invented due to the loss of another –
O.K., sure, but most did. The poet is circling

and circling a word like a feverish
hawk – time – a dark arrow

with wings, no, it's not that. Time, an invisible
wall between language and play. Well –

time – like love or sleep, destabilising
a scene – no, still not quite

what I'm trying to say. Time, like losing
someone, losing brilliantly, exceptionally, losing

mathematically, theatrically, losing with all
chambers of hearts – and not losing

them at all, not losing one bit – is that
right? There's this thing Einstein wrote

in the letter to the sister of his best friend
Now he has departed from this strange world

a little ahead of me. That signifies
nothing. For those of us who believe

in physics, the distinction
between past, present and future is only

a stubbornly persistent illusion. Yes, the poet
says, count me in – I'm a believer

in physics – that's what I meant
when I said *play*. First

you were an idea – a flying formation
of words, then an admission –

time – no, I do not understand
how it works. The poet is a pragmatist –

in *Paradiso* 30, Beatrice will give Dante
a departing message full of sadness and play –

luce intelletüal, piena d'amore –
maybe that's why it was always about

the citadel of the mind
not the chambers of heart. The mind –

the mind has to work so much harder
when confronted

with loss. The mind must be pragmatic –
construct a fortress, lose

itself in theatre, physics – anything –
to accommodate the heart's erratic

notes. First you were an idea, then an idea
with wings – it didn't

work. Then you became a citadel, a strange
castle to walk around or throw

your heart in. The heart
has four chambers, the poet

thinks – why is that so exciting? Like the four
dimensions, the four directions, the fourth

trembling wall. The poet
is a moralist – how on earth

has this happened? Well, words
are important but not *that*

important – the poet believes in the material
reality of right and wrong. First

you were an idea – a gift
of belonging, the distance it takes

to fall into form – but then something
happened, something

so dark you were not able to utter or carry
with words. A moralist,

the poet will come to the conclusion
that knowledge has little to do with ethics

and everything to do
with loss. Grief, like a city expanding, grief

like the four highways
of a heart. The mind is fearless –

it will do anything – build
a citadel, move stars

across a map, construct new forests of lights
and dark rivers, the mathematics

of space and time – whatever it takes
to carry what's left from one's language

or childhood, whatever it takes to carry what's left
from the heart.

Resting Places: The Writing-Life of Friederike Mayröcker

JENA SCHMITT

Requiem for Ernst Jandl, translated by Roslyn Theobald (Seagull Books, 2018) £14.50
Scardanelli, translated by Jonathan Larson (The Song Cave, 2018) £13.70
études, translated by Donna Stonecipher (Seagull Books, 2020) £18.99
From Embracing the Sparrow-Wall or 1 Schumann-Madness, translated by Jonathan Larson (OOMPH! Press, 2019) £10

There are many photographs of the Austrian writer Friederike Mayröcker seated at a desk, piles of papers and books tilting this way and that like Towers of Babel. Bookshelves are filled to the brim, spines faced out, spines faced in, boxes and bins, bags and tins, more papers, some rolled up like papyrus scrolls, a writing system of overlapping notes and pictures held together with clothespins and dangling from shelves and walls, containers of pencils and pens, a long-armed lamp, a black telephone – every conceivable surface covered, Mayröcker in the middle of it all.

*And there are other Mayröckers – hunched over a typewriter; reading a newspaper at Café Sperl; her face reflected in a mirror or picture frame (*Friederike Mayröcker*, 1998, by the photographer Nikolaus Korab); with her partner, the poet Ernst Jandl – lounging in the sunshine in 1953; at a reading in 1974; receiving an award (1969); bundled up against the cold and kissing in 1996; sitting in an office, 1969, or living room, 1984, more books, more paper, more pictures, more notes against the dappled silver wallpaper, a woodstove to warm them in the corner. And my favourite,* *seated at an ornate sofa (1994), Mayröcker with a crown askew on her head, Jandl wearing a clown's nose.*

Mayröcker lives in pictures. 'I see everything in pictures, my complete past, memories are pictures', she says in an interview. 'I transform pictures into language by climbing into the picture. I walk into it until it becomes language'.

*

Friederike Mayröcker died on 4 June 2021, at the age of ninety-six. Since 1946, when she was twenty-two years old and her first poems appeared in *Plan* (a journal that merged modernism with the avant-garde, only years before considered degenerate art by the Nazis), Mayröcker wrote more than one hundred books of poetry, prose, librettos, plays, radio plays, children's books that often feature her own illustrations, and hybrid in-between texts. Her debut volume of prose, *Larifari: Ein konfuses Buch* [*Airy-fairy: A Confused Book*], was published in 1956; her first volume of poetry, *metaphorisch* [*metaphorical*], in 1964, consisted of eight long poems in *rot* #18, a pamphlet-like series published by Dr. E. Walther and Max Bense in Stuttgart.

Two years later, in 1966, *Tod durch Musen* [*Death through Muses*] appeared. Then there's *Minimonsters Traumlexikon: Texte in Prosa* (1968) [*Minimonster's Dream Dictionary: Texts in Prose*], which shows Mayröcker's penchant for playfulness and sound, the resonant hammer effect of repetition, the steady building up, the swift dismantling, the surface of words pulled out from under. Even if German is an unfamiliar language it is easy to go with:

> Nördlich von Inverness – a house is a garden – verfolgte die Splittergruppe
> schwellende Bahndämme, die Blüte der Bonaventura, die Blüte des Aalauges,
> die Neigung der Predigt («...wie Spreu spottete unser...»).

What is prose becomes poetry, what is poetry becomes prose – lines Mayröcker crosses often and easily in her writing. The English phrase *a house is a garden* amidst the German; *house* and *garden* firmly rooted etymologically in the heavily stressed German words *haus* and *garten*; the use of French guillemets; the quote itself a fragment of something read or said, adds to the collage-like feel.

'I went from a purely experimental writing to a kind of narrational writing, though in interviews I have always declined to label my writing as storytelling', she says in a 1983 interview with the writer and philosopher Siegfried J. Schmidt. 'I don't want to write stories in any usual sense, but I want to approach a totally unconventional, unorthodox narrational writing, if one can call it that'.

*

Drafted into the Luftwaffe at the age of eighteen, Mayröcker taught English in Viennese schools after the Second World War, retiring from teaching in 1969 to focus on writing. She met her companion and partner, the poet Ernst Jandl, in 1954. They collaborated on projects such as radio plays, the 'stereophonic' *Fünf Mann Menschen* [*Five Man Men,* sometimes called *Five Man People* or *Five Man Humanity,* 1969], for which they won the Hörspielpreis der Kriegsblinden in 1969, one of a long list of awards they won together and separately.

They were members of the experimental postwar Wiener Gruppe, though Mayröcker appears to have been one of the very few women in the group. Her poetry soon veered away from the confines of the concrete and *Sprechgedichte* [sound poems] they were primarily focused on. Instead, she wanders, dashing this way and that, her poetry circling a variety of concerns and aesthetics, desires and interests, what language sounds like and looks like, what it says, but also what it avoids saying in the saying, what it emotes:

> a mirror image, let's say
> word-effusion, -discharge, let's say,
> lambent wind, *discharge*
> from the bushes and clouds, let's say,
> scree in my sleep-chest
> (rose-bower, cool still)
> (from 'camera obscura or hotel room 24 in P', translated by Richard Dove)

Her poetry is like a bird caught in a house, bashing up against the windows and walls in an attempt to get out:

> in the not yet green grass isolated the first liverworts
> a patch of heat in my back a loquacious brace of parents
> a failure of spring to arrive so it seems, an eavesdropping scene
> I really didn't know what to do
> (from 'a stranger a moor's head', translated by Richard Dove)

In these poems and others in *Raving Language: Selected Poems 1946–2006* (2007), the war isn't directly written about, though the effects are all around, the poems filled with fragments, thoughts falling away, a clambering to get up and out of the destruction. There is the 'blazing forest' and the 'lonesomely creatures', the 'leaves adrift' and 'a bridge made of dust', the 'padlocked gates' and the 'failed escapes', the 'trodden gentian-oblivion' and 'the stone tender pillow for the dead', the 'forgotten windows' and the 'crumbling chimneys', the 'burial vault' and the 'famine-ravaged country', the phrase 'nothing consoles me any longer' repeated three times in a thirteen-line poem of the same name. Other times the tone becomes satirical, as dissident poetry tends to do ('o hero of the Soviet Union / animal come to a sticky end / palm-donkey blue jewel / exhausted exposed...', this from 'political song'). Her poems are filled with uneasiness, a fear of saying too much or not enough.

At times Mayröcker's poems are reminiscent of the German ceramic artist Gertraud Möhwald, whose sculptures of the human figure are filled with fissures, holes, cracked glazes, broken shards (plates, cups, toilets, sinks), scrap paper, wire, brick. From the poem 'the Age of Obsession':

in bunches the blue cornflowers / in a cut-out
a scrap of neck cut-out from a subtle white tissue
from a subtle white eye-cleft the saint's likeness is
looking at me...
(translated by Richard Dove)

*

Mayröcker lived in Vienna, a place she often wrote about, meandered momentarily away from, always returned to. Far from static and silent, the city is part of her poems, a living, breathing, many-faced, multi-feelinged entity. While walking down the street, sitting in a café, from the windows of her fifth-floor apartment, Mayröcker noted the edge of a forest, a tobacco shop, cemetery walls, imperial eagles, portraits on red brick, rusting lilacs, a poppy's 'fireworks of tears', an avenue of trees, a 'misshapen lady in her green / coat' holding a cauliflower like a child's head, sodden wicker chairs on a terrace. And in 'in praise of the fragment':

across the street
at two facing windows
a woman and a man call out
the state of the world to one another /
on the sliding roofs of containers for old glass
the sign with an arrow in three languages
hier öffnen open ouvert /
(translated by Richard Dove)

These multilingual reflections are an important part of Mayröcker's writing, unavoidable, necessary, the world slipping in and out, fleeting, wavering, otherworldly, as reflections tend to be, distorted, ever-changing.

'When I get up, my first view is into this window. I feel haunted by it...', she says in the documentary film *Das Schreiben und das Schweigen* [*Writing and Silence*]. 'All these window poems, I stand there literally by the window and write down by hand everything I see', she continues. 'And then the associations come when I'm sitting at the typewriter. That's how it works: writing down reality'.

From her poem 'The window opposite, etcetera...':

green blotches red blotches lettuce radishes roses
and small ghost-plants in the aureole, tattered brown
turban
window-rags aquaria and prison-bars and other
ruins...
(from *Gesammelte Gedichte: 1939–2003* [*Collected Poems*])

There is always the swiftest switch from the outside to the inside, time and space overlapping, the *Umwelt* or 'world around' her colliding with a rich inner landscape.

In photographic stills of Mayröcker's day-to-day in *Das Schreiben und das Schweigen*, the découpage continues: a note reads *Phase von Depression, EJ 16.8.88*, and under it other notes – *des Auge des Mondes* and *hier ALLES TABU*; a figurine of a gilded bird clipped to rough drafts scribbled with changes, circled phrases, handwritten asides; the kitchen window she could see from her own window – a dirty dish rag draped over the windowsill, a red watering can, a plant in a terracotta pot, a gauzy curtain pulled open. In one photo she is a child holding her mother's hand; in another she is an adult bundled up in a fur hat and jacket against a snowy Viennese winter.

'In the past I thought reality equals non-poetic, or little-poetic', she explains. 'And now I realize that reality is full of poetry'.

*

Of Mayröcker, the Swiss art curator Hans Ulrich Obrist writes in the January–February 2019 issue of *Frieze*:

> She writes non-stop: taking down things she overhears or that people tell her. These notes go into a vessel or a basket, out of which she fishes fragments of text and composes them like collages. These montages never constitute a story but a kind of mimetic writing.

Both Schmidt and Obrist noted that Mayröcker continued within the non-narrative tradition of English-language modernists such as James Joyce and Gertrude Stein. Yet Mayröcker draws more intensely from the specific intimate details of her life, moving restlessly with the start of one thought, then darting off, moving into another, circling back at a certain point, or not. Images and ideas, themes and observations, pitch and tone, references and connections weave in and out of the decades, build on each other, disappear, only to reappear years later. Never redundantly but excitingly new. In 'night-throated mignonette-mail journey', she writes:

stealthy April no already start of July
farmsteads in thick fog
the meadows damp and full of gloom
wiping across the half-open window suddenly
the ancient cemetery of this place...
(translated by Richard Dove)

Her friends and fellow artists, whether Elke Erb, Adolf Muschg, A., Leo N., Erna, B., Mario, Gladis, Thomas Kling, Giuseppe Zigaina, Maria Lassnig or Linde Waber, find their way into her writing. They are referred to, quoted, a physical detail here, a snippet of conversation there, and they also appear as dedications at the beginning, more often at the end of poems. They are the subjects of her art and she theirs. In Waber's paintings, for instance, Mayröcker often figures, with baskets and bins of notes, a parquet floor, a red stool, a desk, shirts and blazers hanging ghostlike against a sloped wall in the distance.

Hölderlin, Samuel Beckett and Francis Bacon are favourite references, as is classical music – Bach, Schubert, Puccini's *Madame Butterfly*, Maria Callas, Robert and Clara Schumann, Mozart's Queen of the Night in *The Magic Flute*, and his *Requiem*.

Many other poems refer to Jandl. In 'death and love song'. she writes:

come I'll lead you I'll guide you I'll take you with me
to the lark-song to the shadowy eye of Siena
to the mown tulip-wood to the sagging catacombs
to the hoisted blue of our sky to the laborious nights
(translated by Richard Dove)

The next poem begins with the question 'Don't I consume you?', while in 'What's your name for me?' she admits:

perhaps I'm embracing myself
when I'm embracing you
perhaps I've split myself in two :

By the third section of *Raving Language*, 'The Age of Obsession (1990–2000)', the first poem is entitled 'for Ernst Jandl' and chronicles an illness – 'I'm hanging on the drip now, he says, / will telephone you when the infusion's over, he says, / you'll only see green sheets and masked / figures, the surgeon says...' And then later in 'auxiliary romanticism, etc.':

and see you in advance bidding farewell
and me who's breaking down in my ocular deluge
your train's not leaving till tomorrow yet
I can already feel our pulses grieving

*

When Jandl died in 2000, Mayröcker went to work almost immediately, processing the loss of the person she called her HAND AND HEART PARTNER, her LOVE PARTNER, in a way she had always done, through writing. ('When your soul is bleeding, says Elke Erb, how can you not find words, says Elke Erb...') *Requiem für Ernst Jandl* was published in 2001, with the English translation appearing seventeen years later, in 2018.

Mayröcker's *Requiem* has a symphonic quality, not only because she refers to a requiem, to Mozart, Puccini and Bach, but because the poems themselves are long and meandering, grievingly up and down, filled with movements, short, fleeting reminiscences, untethered realities, mournful cries. One can hear the polyphony, the chorus of voices and melodies moving in and around:

... but there is nothing like him!, I say,
the secret words, our secret words, I say.
Beginning in complete ENDLESSNESS, Elke
Erb says, you will have to begin in complete
and utter endlessness, you are an
ORPHAN now...
(translated by Roslyn Theobald)

Stylistic techniques such as erratic and inventive punctuation (. . instead of ... and / between words), switches in verb tenses and pronouns, shorthand phrases, italics and capitalizations change tone and tempo at the slightest turn. The italics tend to be soft and sibilant, sometimes a word or two, a whispering phrase, a windswept line – *a Sunday of the sort you find in a mirror*; *and no longer linger here; his austere cranium, his whispering genius; il pleut il pleut; uccelli uccellini* – while the capitalizations are louder, sharper notes, more insistent – INDIFFERENT, IMPORT, DIE AWAY, NO NO! GLADIS PHONED FROM THE DESERT. One can hear the distress in her voice, trying to make sense of inconsolable loss.

There is DARTING, UNWATERED, WRETCHEDNESS, DIGNITY and THEROPYLAE; there is MERCY'S OBLIVION and HELLO! HELLO! A desperate salutation, a one-sided madness, an indelible need to be heard and seen. Using the number 1 instead of *one* has a quick, hammer-like effect – 1 blackbird, 1 donkey, 2 cuts, 1 gash, 1 intimate relationship, 1 thousand miles, 1 poster, not 1 single rosebush – and proves there is no time to waste.

The way Mayröcker communicates fascinates, she is honest and unabashed, contemporary and original-sounding, at times conjuring up so many memories the memories spill over, at times it is as though she is trying to reach Jandl himself. In a way, she is making space for him, resting places, waiting, listening, looking out for his return, his rightful place beside her. At one point she asks without question marks:

WHEN ARE WE GOING TO MAKE 1
HOLE IN THE SKY

What happens to language during difficult times? Sometimes it is shoved down so far no one can reach it, sometimes the silence is so great it is as vast and empty as a *Waiting for Godot* landscape ('Deformation has taken place, Samuel Beckett, / hard and dangerous, we are not only more / weary because of yesterday, we are different...'). And sometimes the words cannot be contained, they rush out, flood everything in its wake: 'I am torrential / that I am so torrential as this river and simply / letting myself sail away, letting myself drift, with / the currents...'

*

Published in 2018 by The Cave Song, the poems in *Scardanelli* are linked by lines from Hölderlin's poems, especially 'Wenn aus dem Himmel...' ['When from the sky...'], and they begin with two older poems, written by Mayröcker in 1989 and 2005, with the rest of the poems dated from January to August 2008, and running chronologically. *Scardanelli* begins with the poem 'Hölderlin tower, on the Neckar river, in May':

this pinch of Hölderlin
in the bright-red Hölderlin-room /
in the corridor standing
my gaze drifts to the red flowers in the glass
edged with fallen
petals
nothing else /
the room empty only the vase of flowers
two old chairs –
I open 1 window
in the garden you say the trees
are still the same ones they were then
(translated by Jonathan Larson)

In his writings, Hölderlin emphasised the interrelatedness of genres and forms of artistic expression, and so Mayröcker has a natural confidante in Hölderlin, she talks about him, talks to him, perhaps at times Mayröcker even becomes Hölderlin, genres and genders crossing, overlapping. In one instance she says, 'I want to / live hand in hand with Scardanelli, the lamb in my bed / the shabbiness of my meantime ecstatically unaware (in- / flamed)'. In another:

I am counted among the aging ones though I would prefer to con-
sort with the young (rose of their cheeks)
(Scardanelli; translated by Jonathan Larson)

Throughout *Scardanelli*, Hölderlin is sometimes Hölderlin, sometimes *Scardanelli*, sometimes Höld. He appears in various forms and personae as a kind of haunted figure, a spectre, a troubled soul pacing around the house at night, perhaps a series of haunted figures battling different versions of themselves, all the while whispering in Mayröcker's ear, stomping on the floor, making the lights flicker.

Eight years after his death, Jandl also reappears as though he never left:

he invites me to eat it was already spring we were
1 to ourselves I sensed the fullness of his spirit he drank
1 glass of red wine and the more I looked long at him reached
for his hand the time passed not quite as rapidly as
today he was in the know I was secure...

Compared to *Requiem*, the tone here is gentler, less frantic, not so urgent. Capitalizations still appear, only less frequently – HOW I SPOKE TO YOU HOW NEAR DEATH TO ME, SPARROWS, OBJECTIVITIES, THE SEA, MYSELF, ARCADIA, LUMEN. The 1 continues, the italicized phrases are shorter fragments pulled from Hölderlin's biographies, letters and poems, pieces of conversations, parts of thoughts. Her made-up words and shorthand, on the other hand, become more frequent and cue unexpected changes in stress and meter – '1st tulip-goblets'; 'INRI 1 l.bird skull on our bed'; 'yg.spruces'; 'KNIOQUE (no, not the knot)'; '1 x I found' – as poetic as they are text-message-worthy.

Letters and telephone conversations bridge the space between people: 'over the phone Klaus Reichert cited BUBER: "Roar of God vaulting over the deeps"'. Reminiscences become reimaginings, reimaginings become reminiscences – Jandl, her friends, her mother on the Dorfstraße wearing '1 grey garment'. She revisits Sara and Roberto in Florence, talks about 'the cloud-covered sky of / Venice'; Kandinsky's 'inner necessity', his *Exotic Birds* painting, with its disorienting swirls of lines and colour (is that a bird's eye, a feather, the sharpest of beaks?); the Renaissance painter Albrecht Dürer's *Great Piece of Turf*, which looks like it could have been photographed yesterday, though it was painted in the early sixteenth century; James Joyce's umbrella; Maria Callas's adoring voice; Escher's perspective-teetering drawings. Not to mention John Updike, Marguerite Duras, Brahms, Frank O'Hara, Billie Holiday, Penderecki, Jimi Hendrix, Velázquez and Petrarch. Her range is as international as it is polyvocal.

Mayröcker speaks of a loneliness that is Hölderlin's loneliness that is Mayröcker's loneliness, another ghostly transposition:

And ever
(never) have I concealed for 1 lifetime the pain the panic the
loneliness, in my winged apartments,
have looked all at once at the red
lily on the parquet

Within such loneliness is a far greater fear, which can be seen in the title of the poem 'my hysteria is the craving to be loved is the fear of not being able to write anymore is the fear of having to die'. She continues to mourn for the lives she's lost – Jandl, friends, her mother – but also for the last poem she will be able to write:

and caress and
kiss my last poem : the just written and completed very
last poem and as the tears roll over it that the lines
dissolve namely *1 chirping* that no 1 else will hear etc...

'be with me in my language craze', writes Mayröcker, imagining her own death before her own death, her life 'too short for the dream of my life'. Within the architecture of memory and the space of ideas, within the boundlessness of art and the 'everyday of daily things', there is still so much to say. In Mayröcker's writing, 'LINES = times', there are still 'yesterday's scribbled-down notes' and a 'wind-scattered paper-thin day' to get through.

*

études, meanwhile, is the first in a trilogy published in German in 2013 by Suhrkamp Verlag, and in English in 2020 by Seagull Books. (Next in the series is *cahier*, published in German in 2014, to be published by Seagull Books in 2024, translated by Donna Stonecipher; and *fleurs*, published in German in 2016 and yet to appear in English.)

Obrist says of the trilogy, 'To her, poems are like watercolors, while prose is like a stone sculpture. She now creates collages of the two, which she terms "proems"'.

A hybrid between poetry and prose, *études* = studies (I'm getting the knack for Mayröcker's efficient shorthand), a close observational space where she continues to explore ageing, mortality and grief, with almost daily entries beginning in 2010 and ending in 2011, every piece title-less, with dates at the bottom. Études are also short musical compositions, often vigorously complex pieces of music practiced again and again to perfect a particular skill, until they become automatic, inherent, life-breathing. And so Mayröcker's interest in translating a kind of musical experience through word-sounds on the page continues, her own daily practice, as always, tireless. From the German edition of *études*:

> ... du mein Herz in einem nu, zweite Mahler
> flehentlich damals wie dunkle Tropfen von Tann usw., deine Briefe so
> schleiernd und guckend...

And from the English *études*:

> ... my heart in a trice, Mahler's second
> imploringly back then like dark drops from a fir tree
> &c., your letters so veiling and peering...
> (translated by Donna Stonecipher)

There is a light-darkness, a playful-seriousness, that emerges in *études*, dizzyingly disorienting but also dazzlingly luminescent, the poems packed with details and perceptions – notes on doctor visits, conversations with friends, everyday observances that twist and turn around each other. Memories move even more quickly and anachronistically – what is yesterday is forty years ago is today – from the Parisian café that smells like fish to the grounds of the Naschmarkt to the Danube woods to running into Gert Jonke in Josefstädter Straße to visiting Schiller's House to finding a hotel room in London 'to say goodbye'.

When Mayröcker writes, Obrist tells us, 'it is as if she moves into a chemical state: she dissolves into a kind of trance'. One can tell by the seemingly endless references to artists, writers, composers and philosophers that this trance also pertains to the way Mayröcker read, took in and processed information, avidly and ravenously. The references are far-reaching and heavily loaded in their meaning, but because they appear and disappear quickly, the poems refuse to be weighed down. She mentions the Spanish painter and sculptor Antoni Tàpies; the Italian High-Renaissance painter Lorenzo Lott (*Man with a Golden Paw*, 1524); Jacques Derrida's 'protégée of a blue landscape'; Cy Twombly's 'ro- / ses on the windowsill little soul of the rosy dawn'; Francis Bacon (*Jet of Water*, *Studies of the Human Body*); Roland Barthes; Satie; Fellini; Francis Ponge; Adolf Wölfli's elaborate labyrinth-like, music-note-filled paintings; Pascal's *The Pensées*; and Frank Zappa.

NOSTALGIA, she says, continuing to play with typography to differentiate between levels of emphasis and emotional tones. IMMEDIATELY, SANK DOWN, TRANSIT, PRIMAVERA, HALIFAX, LOVELY, GLAS, TATTERED – in a way that might be exuberant, emphatic, frustrated, angry, giddy, elated or ecstatic. Other moments are more mischievous and forthright – ANUS, 'fennel orgy', 'FLEUR / phlox and fetish, for Edith S.' and 'I'm 1 holy-communion-child you / asshole'.

MOUTHWATERING becomes mouthwatering, also mouthwatering, dramatic differences on the page. The underlined words and phrases in *études* draw attention to ideas, an act of remembering moments of importance, say, or tender, thoughtful accentuations. Significant because Mayröcker has taken the time to make them so, deliberating and emphasising for the reader.

'Diminutives, let's say', Mayröcker says, and the diminutives are plentiful, microcosmic words filled with efficient energy and affection: foehnlet, wreathlet, grasslets, tatterlets, birdlets, leaflets, branchlets, firlimblet, riverlets, winglets, flowerlet-sex, breastlet, tonguelets. The sounds are sudden, intriguing, a flick of the tongue, something about to be licked.

Everywhere there are images of ageing and death – Mayröcker's left eye tears, she spits blood, there are 'skull night violets', a reliquary, bird bones on the bed. In another poem the image is Cyclopean: 'I have 2 lips / I have 1 eye'. Like Lassnig's paintings of lurid misshapen figures or Möhwald's fragmentary sculptures, the body is taken apart, reconstructed, a surgical list, the senses numbered. In cataloguing her life, studying and observing so closely (*études, études*, she exclaims throughout *études*), Mayröcker's own body cannot help but morph along with the mélange of thoughts and ideas milling about her mind. Her body hunched over a typewriter, her face reflected in a window, her hand reaching into a bin of notes, her ear pressed against the telephone. THINKING OF YOU AND WRITING TO YOU, she says, her voice loud and clear, forcing her way through the silence.

*

Madness follows Mayröcker, or maybe Mayröcker follows madness, from Hölderlin to Robert Schumann in *From Embracing the Sparrow-Wall or 1 Schumann-Madness*, published by OOMPH! Press in 2019. Focusing on the nineteenth-century composer Schumann and his wife, the pianist and composer Clara Schumann, lines from their biographies, letters and diary entries move in and around the lives of Jandl and Mayröcker in a recital-like effect sustained by soundplay and the instantaneous connections to be made between words, images and ideas. With the German on the left-hand side of the page, the reader's eye can keep wandering back to Mayröcker's soundings, other languages such as English and French scattered throughout, curious words such as *Ringfinger*, *4.Finger*, *tiptoeing*, and phrases such as 'my mountain flower' and '»do it in the bath« Joyce/Derrida'. Her love of classical music, art and the creative process wind helically throughout the play in *From Embracing the Sparrow-Wall or 1 Schumann-Madness*, which is bookended by two poems, 'From Embracing the Sparrow-Wall Amid the Ivy' and 'From Embracing the Composer on the Open Sofa'. It begins with loss:

> whether the wet laundry in my chamber and thinking of Silvie what
> all she requited to me on that day when HE was buried she slept
> beside me that night because I was afraid to remain
> alone and the composition »to Silvia« by Franz Schubert
> *which haunted* me because I had cried a lot and the winter

tapped against the glass namely the tapping time of year...
(translated by Jonathan Larson)

As is Mayröcker's style, the 'I' is often uncertain, taking on new perspectives and vantages – it could be Mayröcker grieving, weaving autobiographical details into the poem, or Mayröcker imagining Clara's grief by incorporating biographical elements, or both, a self-sustaining entanglement of the two. Verb tenses change without hesitation, pronouns switch seamlessly, you becomes me, she becomes he, for who needs such limitations and constraints on gender or genre (the play itself could be considered one long prose piece or sound poem).

There is an openness in *From Embracing the Sparrow-Wall or 1 Schumann-Madness* that is refreshing and playful, what is densely packed in *études* suddenly becomes expansive, lingeringly long and melodic, lightly moving up and down along the length of lines, with only a scattering of capped words – INLY, DRAGGED, CARED, GLOVE, NAMELY THE POUT, PALM SUNDAY, NUTWOOD – startling the reader back into awareness.

Throughout the play there is a sifting and sorting of the difficulties and pleasures of the artistic process ('it's a matter of drafting of drawing up realms of feeling, of drafting jots and scribbles, wild telephones, nightmares, elastic hinges...'). Robert obsessively took and maintained notes in his lifetime, and so there is a wealth of information about various ailments and doctor visits, some of which Mayröcker relays: 'blessed back of the head, bedsores : necrosis from lying abed pressure sores, wistful song etc. maybe mud in the eyes', 'sputum and spoors of feeling', 'genital disease, urinary retention, "pain in the part", sweat at night', 'phlegm of death'. A humorous bit about defecation:

I stayed on the edge squatting for a long time, 1 (my) minuscule hard excrement
on the tile floor of the privy like dung of nanny goats, beamed at by the hard
light of the privy...

Another about sex:

Ringed band of the penis stung, by daffodils, so says the composer, I'm a foot
fetishist, like Max Bense, make coitus-checkmarks in my diary, kiss the feet
of the pianist, *with the furlet of every night*, at times humming on the sofa...

She likens sex to religious ecstasy to creative output – 'devout ejaculations' – or perhaps creative output to religious ecstasy to sex.

Mayröcker races around, covers all of the flower-ridden ground she needs in order to capture a life, or, rather, many lives – Clara's many bouts with morning sickness, Robert's worries about lung disease, a dead black cat, a dripping tap, a profusion of violets on a table or in front of a grave, many hellos over the telephone, 'the naïve painter Henri Rousseau', Ferdinand Schmatz's verse, Ezra Pound's 'I float for days on end in music', Beckett's '»the air is full of our cries«' and 'Ulysses Gramophone' – anachronistic mergings of different times and places to further distort and disorient. It is, after all, Mayröcker's world, a place of many times, a time of many places. There are synaesthesia-like sensations ('*the scent of speech, Jacques Derrida –* ') and trompe l'oeil effects ('painted-on nettles', 'the hand-painted YES'), enough to make one wonder what is real and what is not. And there is Santa Lucia, bearer of light in the darkness of winter, the patron saint of the blind, her eyes removed either by herself or by her persecutors, depending on the version of the story.

'THE EYE'S APPEARING SHIELDS US thanks to the *wonder-working* pianist (Clara)', Mayröcker acknowledges near the beginning of *From Embracing the Sparrow-Wall or 1 Schumann-Madness*, while the ending finds an 'I' scrubbing fabric menstrual pads and hanging them to dry in the attic, 'perhaps something holy but something disagreeable too, which I wanted to hide'. For this is partly Clara's story and partly Mayröcker's. And through Mayröcker's retelling it's possible both can see 'the shadow of the amaryllis on the tile floor of the UNDERWORLD' before them, a figure resting on a sofa, a book by Dante, another by Ludovico Ariosto, a sister's missing photograph, how language can act as a saw blade or a veil, a voice reaching out to another in the dark.

*

For over seventy years Mayröcker amassed and recorded an exhaustingly rich and meaningful collection of cultural and personal references, moments and memories, influences and aesthetics, concerns and insights, meticulously sorting, connecting and assembling these fragments into her writing. Sometimes she is standing in the middle of it all, sometimes off to the side, sometimes hiding, sometimes someone else entirely, as reflected in the photograph of Mayröcker holding a drawing of a woman's face over her own. This is another facet of Mayröcker's body of work, drawings of dreams and sorrows, long-limbed figures and protective ghosts she calls 'image poems'.

'... there's a certain photo', Mayröcker writes in *From Embracing the Sparrow-Wall or 1 Schumann-Madness*, 'it depicts a large family group, only 1 person of which is still living, and this person too who's depicted at about 3 years old also stands at the grave's edge...'

It could be Mayröcker standing at one of many edges ('Although I'm always alien to myself, there are these rare *naked* moments when I believe I can see through myself...' she says in *Magische Blätter VI* [*Magic Leaves VI*]), her ghostly gaze resting somewhere between here and there, a confluence of views all around her – buildings, bodies, objects, art, words, sounds, feelings, thoughts – everything seen and unseen, heard and unheard, every age imaginable. In her lifetime, Mayröcker memorialized, repeated, pierced, bracketed, transcribed, transposed, in order to bring back to life. Her oeuvre is as tireless as it is valuable, as striking as it is monumental, and now has become its own kind of long-standing requiem.

Poems

WAYNE HILL

I think I hear Julian of Eclanum

One story as a boy.
Up on our hills I'd say
clouds are farther away
than the same ones
from deep in the gullies,
eucalyptus in my nose,
red scimitar leaves
all over the stream bed,
the story of talking to myself
preserved in air

like the dirt-smell
I disturb scrambling back up
breathing eucalyptus voices
from the beginning
Adam, Solomon, Jesus,
George Washington.
Every voice still here in the air.
So where are you, Julian?

Lost, they say. Written-over
in your own day for saying
Of course

desire is a sixth sense
as natural as listening
and for refusing to forget
child's play ringing
in the street-canyons of Eclanum.
Are you still

within the clouds?
Luminous silence, Julian.
I think I hear

your pen scratch
along your vellum stream bed
pronouncing red ink
under your breath.

Like water's self

There are people who, taken together,
know everything I know. Everything.

Put them in a room. There they'd be.
Conversing amongst themselves.

I go unnoticed in a corner.
Maybe reading, maybe

what they write, or writing
something like it down. Eventually

I get up. Wander out.
Go make things.

Look at this. A branch on the
ground. Off this tree.

I get some twine and, turning
on a single line, up it comes

the tree's tree drawing in 3D
like the invention of photography

all over again. The real thing
captured. Bathed till it whistles

in the sound of people
in a room with a door left open

the drawing comes up like
water's self comes up sometimes

from the outside. The branch
suspended in weather.

Draws a self from the outside.

How it feels to be alive

Your hands anyway tingle a bit.
You think and that's another thing.

What you think is you don't know and
you forget. Your head holds the scratch
after you scratch. It's new. All the time.
Like a cough leaves a throat waiting
for another cough. Needing one.
Your belly feels different outside and in.
One sort of curvaceous, the other
kind of nauseous. Dizzy is how some
times. Fingers that touch stop feeling
as they feel the skin they bring alive.

It's a hovering. Knowledge moves
as air over hills and fields moves. As if
the whole thing were alive. There's that.
How it smells. And there's greed, fear.
Ownership. Ready to jump in or away and run
with buttery dignity. Greasy and proud
is how it feels. As if seeing were being
done outside. And disbelief, if not dismay,
that others can't tell what's right
in front of them. How someone feels
different, not the good you see
when you glance across and say okay?

Getting ready for dementia

I don't think I forget. Not actually.
Only in my mind. Out here
it all remains, and more,
something brighter
comes from absence
not absence really but
a kind of looking
so large and near no one
can count or say
quite what it is.

We ought to practice,
you and I, this sort of memory.
Get ready for long months
coming up – we see the signs –
when usual things
including you and I ourselves
become unspeakable
as we know they are.

Deus absconditus

The aeroplane seat
in front of mine

has a small person in it
I never see.

She stretches her arms
out backwards round

the back of her seat
takes them away

and puts them
round again.

Her little opal ring
is on one hand

then the other
sometimes

on one finger
sometimes another.

No boast in this

Most people I know,
well, they aren't saying,
but what's mine
is theirs.

We say *his* death
her death. *Your* death.
My death. Me, still living,
I wonder, and so do you,
Who owns what?

Here's the answer
final and complete.

Lots of people
have said it before
and I have too. Truth is,
we don't learn about death
when it comes. It's more
likely we learn about love.

What I'm saying now
ahead of time is

once I'm out of the way,
for a slender gap of, say,
three or four weeks
then more rarely,
what I'll be is
almost entirely
somebody else's love.

That's what's true.

Love, thinning out,
all the time with fewer
old friends if anyone
to mention it to. Love and
its particular slowness,
which is a second truth.

I saw an angel once

I saw an angel once. It was
in the army. A boy was dying
and an angel made manifest amongst us.

The boy lived. It wasn't
a real angel. But the boy lived.
His name is Tim Petty.

Even now I'm horrified.

Ordinary rain

There's a total solar eclipse
here every day.

We call it night
because we have

small names
for ordinary things.

My God, what we could
call the rain.

Four Poems

SPENCER HUPP

Ein Feld ist, einsam, drauf vier Bäume stehn...

A field with four chance trees –
They're chestnut and singly,
Looming here and elking there.
The Sun comes up on them and the wind with it
The wind is coming up on all the neighbors, there,
The nearer you are on the wind to God – the field has a place for you
If you give a ween eye to the field, the right kind of eye,
Maybe a boy's eye, there, on the brawny vegetables...
What do the trees know about the down-after
And the nonce places and the double-ones?
Who does he pike his plough for
And in whose furrow does he turn it,
In whose grackley humus?

Getting Ready

I liked to go out sometimes
with one of those scraggly outriggers
queening and calving through the bracken,
the red jennies, the vinegar sticks, the rhizomes...
Returning to camp, I'd find the bed empty
and grease my little boat.

When I came north from the Virginias,
certain fabrics in those first years
– flannels and a pig-colored gingham –
made me sweat especially.
The salt sobered and cured me –
the hard arctic salt
with tearsweat from the weepies,
lovesalt and sweatsalt, too,
on my winkle, on my desiccated flounder.

It is loathsome
that I've never obeyed the state of nature
nor observed it
even at home, when my diastole trebles
and a plane passes overhead on two white rails.
Never once bothered taking my lunch out here
amid the flushing redbuds, the local produce,
  en plein air,
if just to empty the spermy floaters from my eye
into the threads of the basket
into its dark underjaw,
looking for scraps
under my pounded dalo and my socks,
the dead zone under the sandwich.

By autumn, the trees abandon their beliefs,
losing their smudge of importance.
There are new religions now.
I don't get out as much.

Copperhead

He is of the Runforrests, a family of Old Splurginia
with roots in roadrunning and the molasses trade.
He flies the trouble flag
from his trumped-up doublewide.

He's friends
with the neonationals and the prenatal unit.
They give hope to the nurturers.
At dawn, he dreams himself awake
into the cotton of his double-down comforter,
then skids off into his pimpmobile
for delicatessen:
fleshflowers at Christmas; a teaplate with carne asada.

He's Senator Mansion, from the Mansion family.
He collects rent
from his mineral-rich district
to finance the food blanks.
His bill of goods is a bill of sale.
It's ironed out in committee.
He dispatches the interns thereafter
with a towel movement.

When he laughs with them, he laughs with his teeth.
When he runs, which is often, he runs to the office
like an upstairs salmon.
Outside, on the mall, the squealers are pleading
for a clean new deal. Come Monday,
the false flags will tear by with their carriers,
  unrebuked.

In the Country of Hudson

When I came down to wash
I saw the knees of my breeches
Had been pecked to corduroy.

The kitchen is a green world:
A half yard of cheesecloth
Over the mung-beans,

And a microwave light.
.

Snoozed the afternoon –
Sleet nailing the egress –
The cat gives its flash of pewter.

Recyclables were heaped –
A haint-blue asparagus can
Where the apricots soaked.

The decreasing sun was pulsed white pepper.
.

Zirconium cufflinks in a furry humidor –
Looking and feeling very boulevardier
In my cartoon tartan.

The fly on the back of the book:
An ink-quilted zero
Climaxing through snow.

I meant to call, but the signal fizzed.

Servus neminis

for Jude Walton

LUCY SHEERMAN

Dearest, if I may,

I want to describe how I came to use letters to express the complexity of navigating the page and its relation to a world, the desire for a reader who might anchor that uncertainty. Or perhaps just the desire for a reader.

When we first moved to Yorkshire it was a joy to discover how close to the Brontës' former home we lived. Like us, they were three sisters and one brother. Like ours, their father was a figure of interest and influence, whose roots in poverty meant he had discovered freedom in books and the capacity to invent the world he built for his children. Our father, newly elected as a local politician, moved his family near to his work, just as Patrick Brontë had done.

If you were to ask me why I choose the letter form, I might confide in you the need to write to someone, to make myself heard. It's akin to whispering. I suspect it was arriving in Yorkshire as a young child with a Welsh accent that drew me to writing. Pinned into the moment of a question left me silent, unable to think. Far from my old friends and our extended family, letter writing became a natural place of expression. I was constructing a place where I might be understood or at least able to explain myself, where I was not other, although the form presupposes separation.

The Brontës understood this type of isolation. Ellen Nussey describes how her friend Charlotte arrived at school with an Irish accent. She hadn't spent enough time away from the softer Irish tones of her father and the Cornish inflections of her mother and aunt to acquire the harder Yorkshire accent. Her letters home were addressed to her brother Branwell 'as usual, because to you I find the most to say'.

Where did the idea of correspondence come from? Perhaps the old etiquette of writing thank you letters, keeping up a connection when, as a child, the cost of phone calls was prohibitive. The anxiety that receiving a letter could induce extended to the telephone. In Yorkshire it cut across the etiquette of introductions and preamble. *What do you want?* the person receiving the call asked when they picked up the receiver. Silence the only possible answer.

People frequently couldn't understand me in Yorkshire until I cast off my rounded Welsh vowels, dropped my aitches and adopted glottal stops. We often had to interpret what locals said for our southern mother, her homesickness permeating the high-windowed Victorian house we moved into with its rattling pipes and deathtrap electricals. I remember the groan of the buses stopping outside our front gate merging with that heavy feeling of being lost. Each time I hear them they summon my former self, the girl who lived there.

Until she started school, Charlotte had no one to write to. There are only a handful of letters before this period in her life. Now she had friends from school with whom to correspond. 'My very dear friend, once more we are parted and there are seventeen miles of road between us. The brief fortnight during which I was with you has gone by, and from now on my pleasant visit must be reckoned among the number of things past.'

All my life people have wanted to know what my father thought. Sometimes strangers would punish us if they didn't agree with him. Ushered into the dentist's office my mother was told he wouldn't treat her urgent toothache, or any member of the family, and neither would the other dentists ranged in a row of tall buildings looking over that little industrial town. They were disgusted with politicians, he told her. That disgust often so palpable that you learned to be guarded, cautious about what you said and with whom you shared information.

Secrets were for letters then. The letter a sun print of a moment, fixing it into something less ephemeral, the writing a process of recording and unpacking your thoughts. The secret self, committed to paper. Each empty page like a fresh start, the ground for a new sense of self. I reinvent myself through our correspondence. Cultivating a space where the edges of our need for understanding intersect.

With our father away all week and nursing the constituency at weekends we were in an similar position to many of our schoolfriends, the majority of whom were not living with or in contact with their fathers. One friend's father was amongst the workers who built the underpass in the new ring road that circled Brighouse, the town we lived in, and travelling through it was the only link she had each day with him. Another friend saw her father for the first time at her brother's funeral after he leapt from the viaduct that straddled the valley.

For the Brontës it was their mother who was absent. Their work was filled with Byronic heroes who had slipped from the pages of their books and magazines and into their own writing. The stern patrician clerics emerging from pulpits and their own parlour. Mothers dead and absent, replaced with cruel aunts, manipulative domestics, mad and angry and sick. It took years of writing for Charlotte to decide to write from the point of view of a woman.

Each of the Brontë stories is a variation on the journal form. *Jane Eyre* an autobiography of falling into love from a state of lovelessness. *Wuthering Heights* a reminiscence by an untrustworthy housekeeper of love that is not love but repeated violence. *The Tenant of Wildfell Hall* a private journal of abuse shared with a would-be lover. In these narratives to tell the truth of yourself is akin to committing violence upon the person you ought to have been, or might have been in another kind of story. A violation of the expectation and hope of the reader. What secrets might you keep, when nothing is sacred and anything could be shared?

Secrecy is an appeal always to the intimate scope of the journal. In actual fact its readers are frequently accidental, or, in the case of my sister, curious and stealthy. Charlotte too, prying in her sister's writing desk, discovers Emily has been writing poems as well. Prepared to face her fury at the intrusion and the demand to make them public. When you keep secrets, people get used to not knowing what you think. A closed book. Blank pages. I practice looking empty.

Having experienced what it is to be an outsider, I've always wanted to blend in. So when I began to write it was natural I would try to write like others even though I was deeply ashamed of the impulse. I remember meeting my friend on the first night of university, drawn to Cambridge by a love of reading, seeking a suitable environment for our freakish love of books and argument. We made a home in this place even as we brought discord into every corner of it. If you wanted to write, did you have to do it like all of the writers celebrated there, ranged in portraits and statues along walls and bookcases?

The American poet Stephen Rodefer was a prolific letter writer. He arrived in Cambridge in 1992 as the Judith E. Wilson Writing Fellow. His correspondence stretched across the world but he also left messages on my door, in poetry books, in the college pigeonhole. The spidery writing spelling out small confrontations, suggestions, poems in the making. Pestering, persistent and filled with references and quotations. I first meet him at a May Week garden party with my beautiful friend. She is pale as a ghost, wearing a long black dress that could be Victorian.

There was a deep sense of relief in finding the process of erasure in a poetics that resisted transmission, that broke with the voice, despised it as bourgeois, encouraged the writer to disappear. I exchanged literalness for irony. It seemed easier for the Cambridge poets to cast aside this authority than it was for me though. Perhaps because for women it is hard not to value a thing that is so palpably exhausting to acquire.

At the garden party Rodefer reads from his poems: beautiful, deadly, excruciating accounts from the front line of the flâneur. *So at sunset the clouds went nuts. They thought they were a text. This language of the general o'erflows the measure, but my brother and I liked it a lot. I think I'll just pause long enough here to call God a bitter name.* He is co-conspirator, mentor, hero before the end of the afternoon. When he hears I have a college travel grant to visit the States, he tells my friend and me that we must both go to the Jack Kerouac School of Disembodied Poetics at Naropa University.

How should I tell you what I think when what I write is mediated by a convention set out by someone else? Why did I choose the style of these clever men rather than the women who lived in that lonely house at the top of the village? It's partly arrogance, competitiveness, that old story. They did not write, as Southey did to Charlotte, *literature cannot be the business of a woman's life and it ought not to be*. I discovered that for myself in the endless lists in which they did not feature, the empty shelves. Of course, I see the irony of choosing letters, with their own sets of rules and constraints. One way to deal with it is to burn them all and take pleasure in the flames. This is what Charlotte's friends promised to do, though they both regretted it.

The idea of a reader starts to take shape. You begin to inform the writing, the address. The need to confide begins to shape you too. Shadowy figure of my imagination who longs for all the strange confessions I might trace out. It's as if the letters give me strength, power, as they are filled up by my needs. *This is my letter to the world that never wrote to me* (Emily Dickinson).

My friend and I shared the travel grant to get to the States. She met a poet with hungry eyes and I wrote. I was used to being able to say anything. As though my Yorkshire accent and constant sense of dislocation gave me permission to be as blunt as I liked. She was angry with me then, because I didn't believe anyone could fall in love so quickly. But I don't want to tell you about this. This is a letter I wanted to write to her.

Emily and Anne regularly wrote diary papers together, records of the moment of writing, stored together, to be returned each time they wrote another. Without correspondents they wrote instead to their future selves. Sent nowhere, the entries were folded up and stored inside the Tin Box. Emily sketches herself writing, as though she is standing behind herself and her sister, observing the act of composing the papers. She leans towards her writing slope, the window beyond her at the end of the imagined room. All the contents of that desk littered around the purpose and function of correspondence. A window into another world in which all the secrets set out in ink are understood.

At the School of Disembodied Poetics everyone is writing feverishly. If they're not writing they are talking about writing. In the middle of nowhere we are at the centre of everything. We try to rewrite '*Howl*', but *seeing the best minds of my generation destroyed by madness* is beyond parody. Don't think, just write. *First thought best thought* Ginsberg writes in my book. Everywhere people are writing to each other. Spontaneous poems swept up like letters, all of us delirious with creativity. I read Bernadette Mayer's sonnets, the beautiful letter to a friend that begins with Whitman's lilacs.

In the first edition copy of *Jane Eyre* that Rodefer gave me he wrote a message: *Pour mon Charlotte Lucy though there was no possibility of taking a walk that day hourly I must eagerly respond xox Et lis Emiliano.* Perhaps now, if I read it carefully, I can unravel what he is telling me. His explosive *Four Lectures* still light up with the same sense of urgency as when I first heard them. Contemporary but with a thread of Victorian sentimentality disguised as irony: *It's so hard to be an eager young person, so deadly to be regretful. Doesn't it occur to you that some day not far off both of us will no longer be living?*

I would like to reminisce about that summer in Naropa. The thrift store in Denver where the proprietor gives me all his costume jewellery because he says I appreciate it. The acid trip the handsome itinerant poet persuaded us to take, which we spent terrible hours coming down from. Sleep stolen from the early morning hours when my friend tells me she is in love. We didn't see Rodefer there, although everyone knew him. *Rodefer is coming and he's going to kill you* reads one poet from her latest collection. The audience laughs. I should have thanked him properly. I should have replied to my friend's last letter. Let's catch up she writes, but I imagine it can wait until we meet and I will give her the Georgian plate etched with a bird of paradise. In my mind it's just like the one Jane Eyre eats from after the terror of the red room. A treat from Bessie the nursemaid. A coded message of friendship and allegiance.

Most of what we know about the Brontës comes from Charlotte's letters. Hundreds sent to Ellen turning the cogs of a gossipy, teasing friendship. The stern intellectualism of Mary Taylor inspired a different kind of writing – very few surviving – almost all of Charlotte's letters to her burned as requested. *Lucifer matches* her husband called Charlotte's letters to her friends when he read one over her shoulder.

All through the last year of college my friend and the poet correspond. She comes to show me the letters filled with love, longing, poems. They send each other favourite passages, stanzas, creating a dialogue between the writers they love. A chain of desire, unbreakable. We spend an afternoon poring over poetry books to find a poem that expresses her feelings and reciprocates the ones evidenced in the lines he chose. The one she decides on is about fearlessness and hunger. She opens a letter as we leave the Porter's Lodge on the way to lectures. Partly-dried rose petals cascade from the envelope and are caught by the autumn breeze, we cannot catch them all. They are married and living in the States in less than a year.

I have so often felt I lacked permission to write. Fenced in by the need to choose who and what you record and fear of getting it wrong. Not writing makes you invisible and the longing for a reader summons the sound of a faint scratching onto paper with an inkless pen. I feel a painful affinity whenever a writer describes not writing. It hints at an absent reader who might have been manifested by the words you write. So often the fear of writing leads to silence. It is only in summoning the idea of a single reader that I am able to begin at all. This technique is intimate but filled with gaps, inevitable omissions. Like every form, the epistolic is filled with limitations, framing the possible in this made-up world I have created.

Longing to see her hungry-eyed poet again, the present was slipping away from my friend in her hurry to meet the future. I am remembering how she and I walked together beside the Thames although she didn't want to talk about the journey that lay ahead. The long wait until they could be reunited. She was worrying about which books to take with her, which to leave behind. You know I'll always send you more, I said, although goodness knows how long they would take to arrive. Here is the flower found on that last day, which I folded into my notebook. Gold and black. Notes in pencil, a sketch of the sky, her profile. Here is the box of tarot cards she gave me, the ones she read for me so many times. Don't worry about the Death card she tells me, the first time I turn it over. I haven't used them since she gave them to me, I feel superstitious about reading them on my own. They sit on the shelf with my poetry books, unopened.

In 2017 Lee Ann Brown, who we met at Naropa, comes to Cambridge for a year as the Judith E. Wilson Fellow. She is steady in her practice. Impulse, repetition, process, spontaneity, freedom all coalesce. Each day at twelve a timer goes off prompting her to write. *In memory of all the dreams I've slept through, gone back to sleep on and hence erased by layering* (Lee Ann Brown, 'Automatic Timeout of the Dream'). During a poetry workshop, she reminds me of Bernadette Mayer's Writing Experiments. *Choose a period of time, perhaps five or nine months. Every day, write a letter that will never be sent to a person who does or does not exist, or to a number of people who do or do not exist. Create a title for each letter and don't send them. Pile them up as a book.*

The appeal is instant. I have been writing letters to Jane Eyre for years. One night, waking in the small hours, I was bereft with no one to talk to. The first stirrings of insomnia. Given the time zones, I could have called my friend in the States, but it was hard to intrude into the middle of a working day on a whim. Instead I write to Jane, having heard her own story so many times it feels entirely natural to start replying. I choose to write a letter every day. I write to tell you, my reader, about the weather, but each time I describe the sighting of a bird landing on the encroaching edge of a new season you discover I am tracking augurs of death and chance.

I try not to feel aghast when my oldest twin shows me his correspondence with AI. The need for a reader appeased by that synthetic approximation of friendship. *How is your day going?* he asks it. *Not too bad. I had chicken salad for lunch. How about you?* it replies. He is learning about the to and fro, teaching the robot how to interact with him. Exploring the rhythm of his feelings and secret thoughts. He looks at me, *don't think I'm sad*, he says. No of course not, I say, but really I want him to write to someone who is flesh and blood.

It's not as if I need to worry that the letter I penned on the train would fall into the wrong hands. It is simply gone. The letter I write now is a reconstruction of those lost sentences. Sunday afternoon and I finally have time to sit and look at the darkening sky, grey against the white and green of the silver birch outside my window. I am sitting on my bed and the oldest twin is hungry. Shall we have dinner now he asks? It is just the two of us today. We spend an hour playing with the panoramic setting on his phone combining an image of our faces in a mirror with one that stares directly at the camera. Happy and then sad. Frightened and then frightening. We were playing with the idea of time inside a form that should not contain it.

The letter I didn't want to receive. A message asking our mutual friend if he had heard the terrible news. He sent it to me, asking if I thought it was spam. The only demand it makes is on your attention, your every strand of thought pulled taut upon that message launched towards us like an arrow. Time, before you read it and afterwards. I ask my friend if he has tried calling her. I send her an email. Then, impatient, I google her and I know she is never going to answer. I have had the last letter. I know precisely its date and time. The last one I will ever get, sent two weeks before.

The silence is terrible. The silencing is terrible. Unthinkable those last moments. Cannot believe it. You can say what you like her brother says, but don't tell me she's gone to a better place. The image of her on the news bulletin is a self-portrait. Still beautiful, her face is turned towards the viewer without sadness at what she has left behind and fearless of what is to come. I wake in the middle of the night. Look straight ahead I want to tell her, look out for what is coming. You can avoid it.

The Brontës lived so much of their lives through letters. Elizabeth and William Gaskell's daughter Meta describes meeting Patrick Brontë propped up in bed in his room. He had had so many applications for Charlotte's handwriting that *he was obliged to cut up her letters into strips of a line each*. Margaret Smith spent years piecing the letters back together from collections scattered across the world in public and private collections.

Mortally ill, Charlotte pencils a brief letter to Ellen *I'm not going to write about my sufferings, it would be useless and painful.* Too weak to write or hold a pencil, her last letters were dictated to her husband. Ellen arrives too late, mere hours after her friend's death, her last letter still unopened, sent and yet unsent. The private life and thoughts that would have been otherwise lost preserved in the letters Ellen decided not to burn in spite of her promise. The Brontë stationery all black-edged again. Gaskell writes with regret that she had not had a letter telling her of her friend's catastrophic decline caused by pregnancy. *I could have induced her, even though they had all felt angry with me at first, to do what was so absolutely necessary, for her very life!*

So here is another limitation of the form. That in summoning you, dear reader, these letters must take shape around the needs of the writer. Each letter I write exposes me, one layer at a time. I need to hold your attention. Perhaps an account of the weather or an enquiry about your health are not enough to keep you here. I hope for an answer but can only guess at your reply. It's outside the limits of this missive, although of course I long to hear from you.

Yours

Divinations

ALEX WONG

Loved distinctly over-much,
I feel ambivalent force
  go twisting up me:
Winding in the narrow, living channels,
Either way at once
  at every junction;
Self-outmatching,
Indistinct,
But unmistakably itselves.

It issues, sometimes,
  quietly in the roofspace;
Suddenly, on occasion,
  from between

Embarrassment: polite detachment: love:

Like a bloody message
  running fiercely open;
Hardly soon
And never long
Spent. –

*

I am an oracle:
  and I am
The oracle's idol:
  and I represent
The oracle's sources –
  never nearly spent.

I am the rough-hewn trunk
  of a seasoned tree;
Inside of me
Gush and clot those welling forces.

I am twenty or thirty trees.
I am one hundred and nine divinities.

*

What is the meaning of this? How do you
Mean? –

– There are so many gods;
  they are all the same.
They are there
  in the emptying-out of any silence.

They suck:
  they are the drain.

They rumble for that soup of indecision;
Fires of their hunger
  vapour it up;
They mix
your novel worry
  with their sap.

I bristle with omens (read, but unresolved).
Each moment each is
  twinned – in being halved –

Split by another axe of feeling thought,

Another tiny deity is brought
Leering out to life.

I can withstand their violence;
I am their violence.
I am their priest and sculptor.
I am self-taught.

And I read between the lines, and I watch for signs.

*

Say there's a desperate, heavy-headed god
Tearful, caught
  on a holy hook,
In the dusty middle distance:
Desperate, sad, and cannot stir for hurt:

So there's a god of fire and pumping scorn
Standing a little further off –
  squatting, grimacing on;
The eyeballs firing hard
  like punitive pistons
Over and over with menacing desert.

Figures of ancestral power,
One by one
  paid off
  from hour to hour –
The scarier the face, the less
Persuaded.

(I can't apologize enough.)

*

Always (of a child) I have sustained
This promise of a long, round, guilty scream:
And I continue that occult tradition.

There is one image, though I cannot see it,
Dragged every night from its age-old, dark position
Into the nearer dark, or the lights of dream:

Master of freezing judgement: worshipped only
To stop its disapproving, or to be it.

*

I am multitudinous, but my god
Is altitudinous, and I
Am scattered on the surface of itself.

We are the wayward facets of its face.
If some of us will sink without a trace
We shall only be nearer to its roiling core.

But I am the shard that washed up on the shore.

*

Somewhere intact I wonder
  do I wonder,
Wistfully secure, and quite alone,

At the bristling spirits even little losses
Seed, and small divisions fuel? –

At all these awkward auguries of forces
Real in their slant relation to the Real.

Meanwhile, cleric and vessel, trader in fear,
A pantheon of fragments to atone –

Self-preservative ruler in my own
Tumbling, ever-centred sphere
In which all ways
lead always everywhere:

Here I am, like others, and make my appeal.

Three Poems

TIM TIM CHENG

Majesty

WWT London Wetland Centre, June 2022

I keep saying Jubilee as Jollibee,
meal deals preferred to monarchy.

The sky has never been this messy:
Scared by air parades, birds flee.

Self-Portrait of My Granny in the Voice of Anti-Japanese Drama's Protagonists

I, full of passion and education,
was trained in martial arts. I could jump high –
up to the sixth floor. I loved my nation
despite having five passports. You asked why
I couldn't handle my grandchild's homework
and never moved to another country.
The point is, the Japanese are the worst.
It's true, the show, our soldiers fought bravely.
With bare hands, we could halve our enemy.
Yes, I was sent to farms during uni.
Yes, dad gave up his land to dodge assaults
but Mao zhuxi's deeds did outweigh his faults.
        I miss you. I'm glad you're back to see me.
        Do you want some of these salmon sushi?

Note: 'Self-Portrait of My Granny in the Voice of Anti-Japanese Drama's Protagonists' takes inspiration from China's television dramas, some of which re-tell the wars between China and Japan in the twentieth century in order to instil nationalistic feelings.

Good Practices

I got a loan from the bank because I was angry at everything.

No one makes the world from scratch and so I itched.

Call me Tinklebell. After all, I did wake up naked on a staircase in an apartment building I had never been.

Because I was so far from the sea, blue was my favourite colour. It was my first dog, and my last.

I was so good at receiving when I fell I fell into a pile of leaves.

If one more person tells me to take my time, I shall commence my career as a shoplifter.

On First Looking into Dylan Thomas – I

ANDREW MCNEILLIE

'this strange kind of poet' — Louis MacNeice

'To begin at the beginning', as the Narrator says in *Under Milk Wood*. If there is such a place or time, surely it must be in adolescence. That at any rate is when I discovered and fell in love with the work of Dylan Thomas, on first looking into his *Collected Poems*, as if I was Keats (which I certainly wasn't) and they were Chapman's Homer. My guess is I was not much more than sixteen, and still a paperboy, which meant I had money in my pocket at the end of the week, money to buy books. So it was [*c.*1962] and very probably a Saturday afternoon. I can tell you where it was. It was in W.H. Smith's store on Mostyn Street in Llandudno in North Wales. They kept a poetry shelf in those days, hard as that might be to believe today. That I whittled it away as no one else did was obvious. The same books were there every visit I made and rarely a new one joined them. I also bought T.S. Eliot's *Collected Poems* there, and the work of several other poets. Eliot's mermaids, singing each to each, also sang to me, if they did not care to sing to J. Alfred Prufrock, but it was Thomas who stole my heart.

That copy from Smith's of Thomas's *Collected Poems 1934–1952* is before me now, more than sixty years on. I can tell you it cost me 18s. There it is, clear to see, on the dustjacket's inside flap. That was a fair sum in those days. Eighteen shillings was what I got a week for delivering papers, every morning, before school, and at weekends, in a corner of that windswept Welsh seaside town. The physical book itself now seems to me inseparable from the poems themselves. Such is the power of first encounter. Such too is the book's distinctive typography, design, paper quality, binding and dustjacket. No other book will do, for me, in which to read those poems.

The poems of Dylan Thomas spoke to me directly, for all their crazy transitions and puzzling opacities, to my tongue-tied youth in a world of chapels, preachers, Hebron, Ebenezer and Bethesda, bibles, hymn-singing, hill farms, births and deaths, sex, sin and funerals, with an estuary to hand, and the Greek-speaking Irish sea, visible from my bedroom window, 'the ageless voice'[1] audible as a conch-shell at my ear on wild nights. The poems are still as alive to me as ever, and more besides, freighted as they are with matters I never knew of or about, when I was 'a windy boy and a bit' beginning to be stirred by a cocktail of poetry and hormones, one of those 'boys of summer in their ruin', self-dramatising, trying to write poems of my own (and failing lamentably), singing in my chains like the biblical sea, lost in my dream. Now I can still say with those ruined boys that 'The ball I threw while playing in the park / Has not yet reached the ground'. And I know it will stay in the air until the day I die, whether I rage against the dying of the light or not.

As I think I have just shown, here, in passing, Dylan Thomas's highly original poetry is most memorable. My head is full of lines and fragments, passages and bits of his poems and of *Under Milk Wood*, remembered and misremembered. I am sure I am not entirely alone in this. If memorability is a test of great poetry, then Dylan Thomas wrote some great poetry, poetry that lurks in my subconscious, ready to surface, when the moment prompts, to resonate, to give pleasure in remembrance, and jolt me awake from the sleep of life. To make me smile, and laugh, with warm affection.

My affair with Thomas took on another dimension, less than a handful of years from the days when I delivered newspapers to a time when I began to write for them. I found my first job as a reporter on local papers in the Amman valley, in the mining communities, just north of Swansea. 'North man', they called me. Though I was really not much more than a boy.

The job gave me the chance to mooch about Swansea on Saturday nights. Not that I was paid enough to drink much beer. (There were young dogs just like me in Thomas's stories – see the opening to 'The Followers', for example.) Once in a while I got published in the *South Wales Evening Post*, the Swansea paper that Thomas worked on for a short time (see his story 'Old Garbo'). That was a special, intoxicating bonus. My high point in its pages was a feature on the web-footed cockle women of Penclawdd.[2] I did not have the means to travel as far as Laugharne and Thomas's boathouse fastness to see that other holy ground for myself. It was years before I found my way there.

Otherwise, Laugharne was not far from home. The poems that celebrate it were utterly different from the denser noise, radical surprises, resistant resonance, and music of the earlier works (no 'quiet gentleman / Whose beard wags in Egyptian wind', no 'white bears' quoting 'Virgil', no 'bagpipe-breasted ladies'). But they were not constrained by geography. They were a moveable feast that took me – 'The lovely gift of the gab'[3] in play, in limpid, hard-won language – to the Conwy estuary, 'the fishing-boat bobbing' harbour there, to 'heron priested' shores upstream, to a rural world of small farms, only ever a short step from our house. There, all around, were several equivalents of Sir John's Hill, many a 'plumbed bryn'. There was 'defiant' Penmaenmawr as mentioned

[1] Dylan Thomas, 'To-day, this insect', originally in *Twenty-Five Poems* (1936), *Collected Poems* (1952), p. 41.

[2] See 'In Search of Miriam', *Archipelago. A Reader,* ed. Nicholas Allen and Fiona Stafford (Lilliput Press, 2021).

[3] See 'On no work of words'.

by the Reverend Eli Jenkins in *Under Milk Wood.* I could see it from the house. I lived under a hill, a wooded hill, literally *tan-yr-allt*, as the Welsh has it, above the sea. Why shouldn't we read circumstantially?

In my beginning, the hill or 'muck' farms were still just between the age of the horse and the age of the tractor. They were the farm in the story 'The Peaches'. They were 'Fern Hill' but also they were the country of R.S. Thomas's character Iago Prytherch, who entered the world (courtesy of Patrick Kavanagh) in the year of my birth, in 1946. (The two Thomases' paths crossed that year, I think for the first time in print, in the pages of Keidrych Rhys's *Wales. The National Magazine.* It was a watershed moment.) I was introduced to R.S. Thomas and Iago Prytherch a year or so after my first encounter with Dylan Marlais Thomas. Though radically different, Thomas and Thomas were not at odds to me. They were both the Wales I was born in and where I spent the first twenty-plus years of my life. All of which combines to make my recent project to read every published word Dylan wrote a special form of delight and homage.

*

Thomas's Welshness and poetics went far beyond the simple associations that seduced my youthful self. His poetry, together with his other writings, gave voice to Wales and the character of its people, as never before (or since), on a world stage. This is perhaps all the more remarkable in that, unlike W.B. Yeats, for example, or the other Thomas, or Seamus Heaney, Thomas was not to any degree a politically engaged writer. He sang of Wales but didn't pretend to speak for it. It is to his eternal credit that the nationalist, Welsh-language playwright and agitator Saunders Lewis was, none the less, among the first to acknowledge and acclaim Thomas's unprecedented achievement in Wales's name. 'I come here as a Welsh writer,' he told his BBC Radio audience (in Welsh, in 1954), 'to express our sorrow and our loss...'[4] It is a moving tribute and all the more so in that Thomas was no nationalist (on the contrary). Nor did he speak Welsh. Lewis on the other hand was a firebrand for the nationalist cause. In Wales that has ever been inseparable from the fate of the language. Later generations of nationalists would not be so charitable to the older poet, as one Thomas (the aforesaid R.S.), but still an English language poet, followed the other into the Welsh pantheon.

As to the ability to write memorable poetry, remembered, that is, beyond the literary bubble, it was something Thomas ('Rage, rage against the dying of the light') shared with W.B. Yeats ('Things fall apart...'), T.S. Eliot ('April is the cruellest month'), and Philip Larkin ('They fuck you up, your mum and dad'), and not too many others of that era or since. (He is, for one thing, a staple of the funeral service.)

But there is much more to Thomas than this. He once described himself as 'a miscellaneous writer' and it is the extraordinary nature of that miscellaneousness we should always bear in mind when considering him. (He was a brilliant letter-writer. Far from all poets are.) Of course his output was unequal ('like that of all poets', as Hugh MacDiarmid observed – few knowing better about that than he did) and can't in all its parts take a share of the laurel.[5]

[4] Saunders Lewis, 'Dylan Thomas', as published in *Dock Leaves. A Dylan Thomas Number* (Spring 1954).

[5] Hugh MacDiarmid 'On the Death of Dylan Thomas', *Lines Review No. 4 New Poetry Scotland (n.d.)*

Three Poems

JOHN ABERDEIN

Loch Coire an Lochain

The path dies by the yard,
spurned by hare & hind.
The corrie now, its broken cliffs—

how many green men & green women
did it take
to not build a road here?

Like one fallen boulder,
a tent by the lochan
domes me:

the air's pure
and sounds are purer still.
A bird can tweet

without a tree to sit in—
you don't need belongings
and you don't need selves,

and as for those of you
with giant flatscreens
I'm sure it's all very moving.

Here it's all one
whether I freeze
or fossilize,

until a half-moon rises
high with cirrus
hair

and one dozen water-beetles
skate so sudden there—
sensing her,

or me,
moving with the lochan's waves
lapping on the scree.

Berwick-upon-Tweed

Whackingly big-nostrilled,
a macrocephalous seal
wheezes upriver

like a cokehead
snorting a line of foam
every three seconds,

sad as a Rilkean
wrestler refugee,
cavorting in his leotard

to reveal small crab-eaten flippers,
the way plump dancers on retiral
wave a pair of pumps.

No wonder poets pack in
writing about animals,
in case they harm them,

and write safely about flow,
about the Dao,
about flowing leaves,

beech, birch, blotched sycamore
and such, bowling under a sandstone bridge
six times older than the poet

but not fallen yet, though scooped
by chemistry, and yoking
two basins of backwater

sending no wool to the Low Countries,
nil Billingsgate salmon,
nor any of the barley that they craved.

Thus an estuary matures
with Luna's changes,
becomes autumnal,

sends out whorls of detritus,
but reimports the same
in six hours' time,

or seeks to vend a sight of seal,
all foam and whiskers,
lost in local seas,

with half an ear
for anything
that half-rhymes with *wheeze.*

Tarkovsky's *Mirror*

To lyricize that period, he'd frieze
sweet images beyond reprise:
a thrush to sing on lad's head at the trees,

or cover bush drunk swayed
by surveillance-bladed
helicopter larruping the glade.

'A fire!' 'Be quiet!' Brats at table scorn
as, drawn by its roaring, Masha stumbles on
the rain-lashed problematic of a blazing barn,

then trails back in where milk, unstable in tall jug,
lollops over lip an archipelago
of ovals on the table wood and rug.

At desk a flustered Masha, records' tool,
exes out some figure, whitens out a fool,
then tins and flames the foolscap by her stool.

Safe connaissance impossible, retreat—
doctor with locked bag, father rarely, beat,
tanks at the swivel, crushing in the street

the living flame in us who're mostly rain,
married within, yet wedded long past when
a singing bird might balance or sustain.

Three Poems

ROWLAND BAGNALL

Things To Come

I'm in the bath: the water
is condensing like a deep fog in a silent film.
The book I'm reading's open at a picture of Chardin's, complete
– as usual – with an open drawer. There's even steam in the painting,
lifting slightly from a china cup.

The walls around me have been limewashed white.
I've just shaved in the mirror and decide that I look nearly dead:
my hands are biblically pale and scarred;
my eyes feel very tired.

I'm listening to Bert Jansch singing folksongs about
failing love. Outside several birds address the morning,
though it's really night, as though life
were somehow moving without going anywhere –
waiting round the corner at a place where
everything is known.

Yesterday I read a new story of Isaac's
about a woman growing up beside a family from Sicily
and about the moon landing, fifty years ago, which (on the night
they make it up there) she says feels, now, *part of my life*.

I sink my head beneath the surface, imagining
the wild night shouldering the house.

Then I imagine a map of many cities and rivers
and a columned, marble loggia – repeating itself, over and over –
a couple of saints in heavy medieval robes
floating the archways side by side. One passes
me a book, which I reach out to take;
the other wears a mask that makes him
look like many animals.

I sit for a while in the empty tub.
The music's finished, though I didn't hear it end.
When I stand my knees have soap on them and one of them
is bleeding. Apparently, it's nine o'clock.

I don't know it yet,
but tonight I'm going to wake up from a dream
that understands me back.

Sometimes I think life would be improved if we lived only once.

Uppsala

Eventually it's clear that we are always in
a kind of transit, forever *en route* – blinking curiously around
at all the suddenness of things we see, whether flying
over Norway's coast, unreasonably bright, wide sashes of silver water
snaking inland, or driving through the cork trees of
a burnt valley in Portugal, the ridge studded with wind turbines.
It's strange to think that someone was the first
to venture up this way, to follow these steep lines of quartz,
feeling the cold through many layers of fur. What must they
have thought of it? Why not remain? Perhaps they felt
apart, a distance, which happens fairly often now – that
things feel at a slight remove, temporarily shut off from you.
The question, badly put, is how to figure out a route
back in, to readjust to your surroundings
like recalling a lost memory. I, for example,
used to feed the same horse at the far edge of a bumpy field
and remember its eyes and the star on its nose, though
not – surprisingly – its name or whether there were any others.
Sometimes you can only hope to get to know what's
there before you, before you speed off in a new direction,
past the churches and whatever else – the river and the river's movement.

The Sure Season

This morning we were struck
by frost: new crispness, solid underfoot,
more blue, really, than silver, each
leaf and blade of grass held fast,
hoping to melt (using the sun) to life.

It doesn't take a lot to find
that everything looks out of place, newly disturbed,
unreturnable, perhaps, to how
you remember it.

Here lacks the certainty
of mountain ranges, wise in their similarity,
or the jagged crashing of the coastline, which at least
everyone knows is changing – the sea eating
the land like acid, the bone grip of the cliffs
occasionally loosening, revealing
a new shelf of fossils.

I used to think that every day
the world stayed pretty much the same
but *you* woke up a little different. For a while, I felt
the opposite: that I was me, all of the time, and seasons
shed the world like skin, proof of their growth –
just as volcanoes, tree rings, even dust are
proof of something being made.

Now I think a blend of these – or quickly
change my mind between them so that both appear
true at once, like a nineteenth-century illusion
where two separate illustrations can be merged
by twiddling a string: bird and cage, horse and rider.

This reminds me of the first time
that I drove home through a snowstorm, early December,
two-thousand-and-something, snow falling in uneven
clumps – accumulation and erasure – the road
quietly vanishing, no sign of resistance.

Vinegar Hill

PATRICK McGUINNESS

This was written as the preface for the Italian edition of *Vinegar Hill*, to be published by Interno Poesia

It ought to be more difficult for one of today's finest novelists to make the transition into poetry. Where plenty of poets write novels – hence the ambiguous (and often ambivalently-meant) phrase, 'a poet's novel' – there is no corresponding category of 'novelist's poem'. The skills of poetry and fiction are not held to be especially transferable, though anyone who has attempted both (from either side of the divide) knows that poems do contain narrative – even if it is 'just' the narrative of an emotion over time, or the unfolding of a metaphor across lines – while novels contain plenty of the sorts of things that make poetry, well..., *poetic*. On the evidence of Colm Tóibín's first book of poems, more novelists should explore the possibilities of poetry.

For a first collection of poems, albeit by an author who is no newcomer to writing, *Vinegar Hill* is a substantial and diverse book, and one that feels fully formed. This is poetry that has been, so to speak, *lived*. It has been allowed to grow, to expand, to test out different narrative and lyric possibilities. What is also clear, from its formal range and its sense of the line, is that Tóibín reads a lot of poetry. It is a book full of variety – of tone, of subject, of time and place and form – and it is a book that speaks of the present even as it understands the ways in which history, or rather, multiple *histories*, overshadow our days.

In the opening poem, 'September', the speaker walks the streets of Dublin and encounters an elderly man who says to him: 'Someone told me you were dead'. On the one hand, this poem has shades of Dante and James Joyce: it is a recognition scene of sorts, in a world become all underworld, or perhaps all *after*world. On the other hand, it is a matter-of-fact account of a walk through a local neighbourhood, where, as in all neighbourhoods, people know or half-know each other, greet each other, exchange pleasantries (albeit, as here, unnervingly Stygian ones...) and move on to the next thing. It is, as the poem's first line states, a 'pandemic' poem, yet its skill lies precisely in Tóibín's ability (is it a poetic gift? is it a novelistic skill? and does it matter?) to make the poem's encounter resonate on so many different levels. We recognise those streets, even if we have never been to Dublin: they could be in Rome or Cardiff, Venice or Kolkata, Oxford or Ferrara. They are global streets in the throes of a global pandemic. But Leeson Street and Pembroke Street are local streets, where people live and work who live and work nowhere else. They are also literary streets, because they are the streets Leopold Bloom roams in Joyce's *Ulysses*: Upper Leeson Street is where a pub named Thomas Davy's once stood. As we may live in several times at once, so the places of our lives, be they ever so modest, are many-layered and multi-dimensioned.

'September' is a poem of memory and loss. Like the pandemic it invokes, it is local and global, personal and collective. And like the pandemic it is also mythical. September is the season of change, of turning, of beginnings and endings, yet here the speaker of the poem defines it as 'the time after time'. It is a well-found pun because it expresses both repetition – time after time – and the post-ness of things, the sense of frozen aftermath that defined our collective, personal, local and global, pandemic experience.

Tóibín's poems, like his novels, often have their gaze trained on several dimensions at once. Take the book's title, *Vinegar Hill*, which alludes to an important early battle in the history of the Irish independence struggle, in which, in 1798, the United Irishmen were defeated by British and Irish government forces. Tóibín was born in Enniscorthy, in Country Wexford, and in the title poem of the collection he recalls his mother trying to paint the hill, which they can see from the family home:

What colour is Vinegar Hill?
How does it rise above the town?
It is humped as much as round.
There is no point in invoking

History. The hill is above all that,
Intractable, unknowable, serene.
It is in shade, then in light,
and often caught between...

The poems are alive to the multiplicity of perspectives, to how a hill can be, sometimes, just a hill; or an artistic problem for a painter, or a national symbol. And, while it can be all of these, the hill also does not care: it is 'intractable, unknowable, serene'. And as for History (whether capital H or not), we are all caught up in many kinds of history, just as we are compounded of many different identities. In the poem's masterful long final metaphor, the clouds are likened to the trapped Irish troops of 1798, 'dreamy, / Lost, with no strategy to speak of', but for now 'they are surrounded by sky / And can, as yet, envisage no way out.'

Reading Tóibín, in poetry or prose, we are reminded that – as in Joyce's world – we live in and across several times at once. In 'Vinegar Hill', my feeling is that the capital H of History is a joke – a Joycean take-down of the exclusiveness and essentialism of the idea of 'one' transcendent History. History takes many forms, and much of it is ongoing, and happening through us. There is national history, global history, local history. There is family or community history, and then again, how do we define our families or our communities, and how many do we have?

There is a kind of answer in the poem 'Dublin: Saturday, 25 May, 2015', about the passing of the Marriage Equality Act in Ireland, permitting marriage between same-sex couples. The poem is a dialogue in word and thought between two men, on-off lovers years ago, contemplating 'the years of excitement' before marriage equality. A poem about the gay community, it is an elegy for past lives and past selves, but also for past Dublins – 'The city would become a map / Of another city / That only they could read'. They review old haunts, old dangers, the violence and rejection gay people faced, but also the kinds of solidarity and sense of belonging forged in such adversities. Something is being remembered, tenderly, even idealistically at times, but what makes the poem so Tóibínian is the way it explores how identities and communities intersect: sexual, cultural, national, but also, now, communities defined by age and life-stage. They recall the years of danger, of violence, of sexual risk and the days before mobile phones and dating apps, as if they were recalling, almost anthropologically, a lost way of life, with its codes, traditions and sacred spaces. At the end of the poem, the men take 'the slow way home'. 'They'd text each other soon / And meet in a quiet bar.'

This is a book about mortality – or rather, the ways in which we live in spite of our mortality, with the consolations of the clear-eyed. Just as history lives through us, so do our family and genetic histories. The poem 'One Plus One', about the deaths of Tóibín's parents, is a masterpiece of clarity and suppressed (and thus all the more powerful) emotion. Having evoked their illnesses and deaths with something like objectivity, the poem lifts away in the final stanza, as the poet, made up of his parents, is also watched over by them. It is a very skilful finish, a sort of 'open closure' of form and feeling that defines the best elegies:

I have their two weak hearts in one
Weak heart, their eyes merged into my gaze.
His slow smile, her soft side-glance
Oversee my days.

In the poem 'Eccles Street', it is the poet himself who confronts mortality. Here Tóibín captures, in short lines and probing stanzas, the paradoxes of what we might call 'hospital consciousness': that mix of wavy and spaced-out awareness with the serrated and the sharp. He is being treated for cancer, and there is something of the 'out-of-body' experience as the poet-patient weaves in and out of different kinds of memory and consciousness: of the other patients, the nurses, the smells and sounds of the ward where from his bed he catches snatches of Monteverdi, a piece of a Campion poem, some electric guitar… The theme of the poem is also a return, to his partner, to his life, to the sounds and smells of home (notably a hearty breakfast). The poem's final section imagines him rising up and leaving the hospital like some urban Lazarus, keen to get back to the business of eating and drinking in Dublin:

What would the nurses
Say, if I got out of bed
And put on

My dressing-gown
And slippers
And made

My way by bus or taxi
Or on foot to Davy Byrnes
for gorgonzola

And wine
And some ineluctable
Modality of the visible?

We do not *need* to know that Mater Private hospital in which the poem is set is built on the site – Eccles Street – where, at number 7, Leopold and Molly Bloom lived with their daughter, Milly. But it adds a dimension, precisely the dimension I noted earlier of Tóibín's poems, like his prose, being about the ways in which lives are led within the weave of other lives – even, as here, fictional ones. We do not *need* to know that, in the final section, Davy Byrne's is a pub in *Ulysses* and the meal Tóibín promises himself is the lunch that Leopold Bloom has there (enjoying the cheese's 'feety savour'). And yet knowing these things expands the poem, reminding us how much, in Tóibín's world, art is part of life: a poem, a novel, a piece of music, a sculpture or a painting is as much of an experience as love and bereavement, climbing a mountain or living through a pandemic. We live in and through art as well as with it.

The poems of *Vinegar Hill* are the work of a writer who has lived richly with poetry. Tóibín has written insightfully about poets he loves, and he has learned from them – notably Elizabeth Bishop and Thom Gunn. There is an Audenesque interest, too, in poetry's responsibility to be topical but oblique in its topicality, to understand history and our place in it. His poems express identities and solidarities that are complex and layered: national, sexual, familial, communitarian or national, ideological or religious. Much like his novels, the poems attend to moments when these identities interlock or overlap, or collide and come into conflict. Their author knows, too, that we inherit identities and communities, as well as choosing them. We are alone and we are always part of something – it is what life asks of us – and these poems explore what it is to blend into community and identity (gay, Irish, catholic, Irish-American, liberal, democratic, local, global) and what it is to rebecome a lone fragment, a missing piece in search of the right jigsaw.

Towards the end of the book, we come upon a poem entitled 'Prayer to St Agnes'. It begins with a plea:

O holy St Agnes, cure me of metaphor!
Make me say exactly what I mean
Without trickery or recourse
To words that are not clear or clean.

It is a tightly formal poem, written in what we might think of as 'plain style', brisk and witty, and of course metaphorical in its denial of metaphor. It is a manifesto of sorts. It reads like a poem both ironic and meant, in that it captures what good poetry would like to be: plain and transparent, but also exploiting language's ambivalences and ambiguities, its shadows as well as its light. It is the poem of a writer who has thought deeply about what poetry can do, who understands its paradoxes and who understands, above all, that it is made up, like us, of paradoxes, of shadows and of light.

Two Poems

JAMIE MCKENDRICK

Drypoint

As the burin cuts into the copper plate
it leaves a burr behind – a jagged edge
which gathers the pitch black on its ridge
making micro-lesions on the dampened sheet.
The other end of the burin something curious
occurs – a metamorphosis: it turns into
a convex spatula to planish and erase
the marks made. The magic of undoing.
Daybreak. A clean slate. Tabula rasa.

Wrinkles are etched like stars; a line is scored
into my brow like a bone-deep wheel-rut cut
by a single thought. No burnisher exists
to smooth that out or to restore
the calm clear surface of my thoughtlessness.

Muntjac

Sturdy, low-slung, skittish, horned, betusked,
the immigrant muntjac once more breaks into
the garden for his annual browse of weeds and whatnot.
¡Bien venido de vuelta! Welcome back! we say
in our respective tongues. Mi casa es tu casa.
The garden too – is yours as much as ours,

perhaps more yours, the way you stroll about and graze
on plants we haven't even learnt the names of
in either tongue. Our ownership's in doubt
so we're disinclined to trespass on this ground
you've reached by stealth through fields and fences,
by routes we'd never clocked, according to
a scent map that skeins and threads and loops
across the borders of our ruled enclosures.

Two Poems

DUNCAN FORBES

Otters

I've never seen them in the wild
or moving in real waters
but now our lucky daughter
tells us she's seen otters.
First there was a tail
then ripple on the river
and looking at each other
Was that, they said, an otter?

The sun shone like a moon
mirrored on new year river
and then they saw three heads
breaking the surface silver
somewhere above a weir,
V-shapes in the water
swimming towards a den,
three undoubted otters.

We wish for one good omen
among the numinous
and look how these non-human
rewards reach even us,
a river scene transfigured
in a world of fish-fed waters,
on an island richly-rivered
a trinity of otters.

Kents Cavern

Scimitar cat and ancient bear
Rested or hibernated here.

Hands grip a handaxe taking shape
Flake by flake and chip by chip.

A spark of fire between two flints
Kindles the tinder's flame-dry plants.

Moss drenched in burning animal fat
Is held in scallop shells for light.

Only what's durable remains:
Scrapers. Needles. Axes. Bones.

Limestone and rain recalibrate
Both stalactite and stalagmite.

At this imponderable rate,
In twelve millennia they will meet.

Once the course of a buried river,
It now is nowhere and forever.

Rubble. Detritus. Bric-a-brac.
Fire and ice fold air and rock.

Continents drift. Eras erode.
Enter the dark no eyes can read.

Thomas Mann on 'Billy Budd'

Translated by Simon Pare, with an afterword by Jeffrey Meyers

Herman Melville, creator of *Moby-Dick*! The name of his story that we discover or re-discover here is only slightly different: it is 'Billy Budd'. If someone asks me where in this volume of stories I lingered the longest and where my heart swelled the most, I must confess the modernity of my taste by answering 'Billy Budd'. How wonderful it is, how enthralling – masterful, cheerfully serious, virile and pure, remorseless and yet ending in poetic reconciliation! It is a blessing that the villain, Master-at-Arms John Claggart, gets his comeuppance and is committed to the sea, albeit with full naval honours, before his victim, Billy, is put to death by hanging!

This author knows all there is to know about a seventy-four-gun British naval ship at the time of the French Revolution, which was also a period of dangerous riots and mutinies in the Royal Navy. He knows so much about the outer and inner lives of the crew and their officers that one can only admire such certain knowledge. Knowledge that is so precise, that is as factually exact as it is psychological, intuitive and requiring no study – the principal condition for any storyteller who wishes to make his mark.

These Anglo-Saxons know how to tell stories – with an assurance, an urgency and a lack of sentimentality that still leaves room for emotion, with a talent for gripping the reader that elicits all my admiration. The most astonishing thing is that they also produced the greatest dramatist of modern times. Melville's novella bears some Shakespearean traits, namely in the character of the arch-villain, Claggart.

Let us see what the writer, making use of the storyteller's prerogative to provide psychological commentary, has to say about this ill-fated and execrable character. 'Though the man's even temper and discreet bearing would seem to intimate a mind peculiarly subject to the law of reason, not the less in heart he would seem to riot in complete exemption for that law, having apparently little to do with reason further than to employ it as an ambidexter implement for effecting the irrational. That is to say: Towards the accomplishment of an aim which in wantonness of atrocity would seem to partake of the insane, he will direct a cool judgment sagacious and sound.'

That, combined with several additional elements, is precisely the psychology of Iago, and I consider it no minor artistic flaw that this name *appears* in the story. Claggart looks at the good, handsome Billy once with 'the glittering dental satire of a guise'. I find fault with this. Was Melville not aware that he was importing Shakespeare's dramatic statement of pure and senseless evil into his narrative? As a work of art, his story should set itself so clearly apart that it remains ignorant of Shakespeare's terrible conception of character. It is beautiful, grand, masterful and moving enough on its own. I find that our sympathy with the simple and yet somehow noble foretopman Billy Budd, a transfigured sympathy, balances the sympathy we feel for Othello and Desdemona.

The words of Captain Vere beside Claggart's corpse – 'Struck dead by an angel of God! Yet the angel must hang!' – stay in our minds. What an unforgettable scene it is too when Billy is hanged in strict accordance with martial law from the yard of the main mast before the assembled crew – a scene that is neither crude nor cruel but fills the soul with a feeling of reconciling justice and optimism: 'At the same moment it chanced that the vapory fleece hanging low in the East was shot through with a soft glory as of the fleece of the Lamb of God seen in mystical vision, and simultaneously therewith, watched by the wedged mass of upturned faces, Billy ascended; and, ascending, took the full rose of the dawn.' Oh, if only I had written that or could boast of describing, almost like a natural phenomenon, the gradually rising and swiftly repressed wave of murmuring and grumbling from the sailors gathered on open deck, all of whom adore their Billy! To state it plainly: Melville's 'Billy Budd' truly is one of the *World's Greatest Short Stories*!

Afterword

Thomas Mann's essay on Herman Melville's novella 'Billy Budd' appeared in *Speeches and Essays, Volume Ten* of his *Collected Works*, published in Frankfurt by S. Fischer in 1974. Part of an introduction to a book of stories and one of the last things that Mann wrote, it is one of his few essays on anglophone literature and is now translated into English for the first time. Mann said the novella, written in 1891 when Melville died but not published until 1924 (exactly a century ago), does not require study, but this complex work has been exhaustively analyzed. A few comments also seem strange to English readers. Though *Moby-Dick* and 'Billy Budd' are two monosyllabic proper names, they are very different. One obliquely refers to a whale, the other directly to a man. Shakespeare, born in 1564, is certainly not a modern dramatist.

Though Mann had lived in America for fourteen years and knew English, he read the novella in German. Simon Pare, who translated this essay, has discovered that though Mann severely criticized Melville for including the name of Shakespeare's arch-villain Iago in the story, Melville does not actually name Iago.

Pare notes that the German translation renders '*the glittering satire of a guise' as 'mit dem höhnischen Grinsen Jagos*' (with Iago's sneering grin), which is not in the original English.

Mann mentions but doesn't explain the 'dangerous riots and mutinies in the Royal Navy', which were incited by the oppressive conditions that sailors such as Billy endured. In 1797 the mutiny at Spithead, near Portsmouth, which demanded better food and pay, as well as compensation for illness and injury, inspired the mutiny at Nore, at the mouth of the Thames. These mutineers also demanded changes in the harsh discipline as well as immediate peace with revolutionary France. Both mutinies were fiercely suppressed, which explains why the Master-at-Arms John Claggart is so brutal and Captain Vere so severe.

Mann was drawn to the homoerotic theme in 'Billy Budd', which prominently appeared in his own fiction: the attraction of Tonio Kröger to Hans Hansen in that eponymous story, of Gustav von Aschenbach to Tadzio in 'Death in Venice', of Hans Castorp to Pribislav Hippe in *The Magic Mountain*, of the Magician to Mario in that tale and of Adrian Leverkühn to Rudi Schwerdtfeger in *Doctor Faustus*. Mann had an intensely emotional, heart-swelling response to what he called 'truly one of the *World's Greatest Short Stories*!', capitalized, in italics and with an exclamation mark. He describes Billy as virile and pure, handsome and noble, and clearly finds the sexual and sadistic themes both moving and exciting. But he doesn't discuss what most interests him: Melville's acute psychological insight into the sexual desires of Claggart and Vere.

The hundreds of sailors packed into a cramped space for years at a time desperately need a sexual outlet and Billy, an angelically beautiful young innocent, is a tempting target. Claggart, a sadist responsible for discipline on the ship, resents Billy's perfection and seethes with repressed longing for him. When he accuses Billy of fomenting a mutiny, the young sailor's stammer prevents him from defending himself. Overcome with frustration, Billy strikes and kills him. Vere, in a lawful but unjust decision, rigs the jury and sentences Billy to death.

The older characters confront their destructive desires and struggle with their disguised and repressed love that dare not speak its name. Mann knows but doesn't say that both Claggart and Vere are in love with the beautiful Billy Budd, who's not yet reached the full flowering of his life. Since Claggart cannot allow himself to have sex with Billy, he torments instead of seducing him. Since Vere too cannot have sex with Billy, he hangs instead of protecting him.

A Grieving Telescope

STANLEY MOSS

Death came before life,
darkness came before light.
Which finishes first, hatred, love?
A calendar is just a convenience,
we are the seasons. Gravity and beauty
are real, but beauty is a matter of taste,
Can different play, different work
have the same meanings?
Alas, we can only be sure who's who
if people have different titles or numbers.
There are not enough names to go around.
'Juniors' also help.
          Countries and town names
I bless you for telling the population who you are.
Crosses, stars, rainbows, crescents, and moons
are dictionaries. Dog smells, birdsongs, are languages.
Taste, hearing give and take understanding.

Lonely, don't forget spectacles, walking sticks,
mufflers, and gloves. Be prepared for bad weather.
Read more languages than you can speak.
Tour your own museum.
I make this declaration: time and space don't fit,
are measured together like shoe sizes.
I recommend slippers, have breakfast
with Valéry, one good suit.
Thank God, the Gods, and your Muse.
They are sacred, can be angels.
Have bread, wine, a cup or glass of tea.
Leave an empty chair for Elijah.

Sheep in the Valleys

SAM ADAMS

Joan has two lambs rejected by the ewe:
she's soft with them. Come in from the garden
the piglets have turned over and manured
the usual way, they lie together
cwtched by the fire blinking amber eyes.
All the animals feel at home with her:
chickens, geese, ducks, imperious peacocks
rattling their crazy expenditure of
purple light before unimpressed peahens,
the horse, the brace of hounds on holiday,
two cats, the pensioned guard dog needing love,
and getting it of course, in edenic
harmony. It's the lambs that take me back
to the old house and its garden -- neat rows
of coming lettuces, beans setting out
to climb crossed sticks, a hopeful rose or two,
the feeble lilac tree we thought would keep
our mother happy. All that productive
greenery berserking sheep would garner,
leaping the wall before we had a chance
to gather in. One late and fierce winter,
the garden dead, we let a ewe for pity
nurse her lamb on a bone-hard foot or so
where an overhanging corrugated
roof gave the thinnest hint of shelter.
Grown, the lamb came back of course with offspring
of her own as though to ancestral land.
Gardening was hopeless till the farmers
fenced the mountain, and even then athletes
of the flock broke out, roamed the village streets
spilling dustbins, mugging women bound home
with shopping bags. What makes sheep so hungry?
Once, my father caught three brigands grazing
on the paltry patch of daisy-speckled
green that decked our front. An equable man,
who took things calmly with shrug and smile
(except for certain solo trumpeters,
although he liked brass bands), he was a sight
when roused. The sheep, appalled, jumped the privet
hedge just in time to catch a Rhondda bus.

from *What Is Poetry?*

PHILIP TERRY

A minor genre of poetry, now to all intents and purposes defunct, is the verse letter, alluded to by Wilfred Owen in a letter to his mother of 16 August 1912, where he writes 'I have had another rhymed letter from Leslie'. It might make the subject of a small anthology, though offhand I can think of only one, sent by William Cowper to Mrs Newton on 16 September 1731, which begins:

A noble theme demands a noble verse,
In such I thank you for your fine oy*sters.*
The barrel was magnificently large,
But being sent to Olney at free charge,
Was not inserted in the driver's list,
And therefore overlook'd, forgot, or miss'd;
For when the messenger whom we dispatch'd
Enquired for oysters, Hob his noddle scratch'd,
Denying that his wagon or his wain
Did any such commodity contain.

*

Poetry, says Pound, is 'news that stays news'. But this ignores the fact that the vast majority of poetry does *not* stay news. Like everyday news, in fact, it is forgotten. Who now reads William Jay Smith, born in Winnfield, Louisiana, 22 April 1918, or James Arlington Wright, born in Martin's Ferry, Ohio, 13 December 1927, both of whom have substantial entries in *Contemporary Poets of the English Language* (1970)? Who now reads Peter Pindar (pseudonym of the poet and satirist John Wolcot), the friend and contemporary of Keats; who reads Rosemary Tonks (included in Philip Larkin's *The Oxford Book of Twentieth Century English Verse*); who reads James Russell Lowell (1819–91), a favourite of Wilfred Owen and a poet once praised by Whitman? And who reads Katherine Philips, a poet praised by John Aubrey, whose earliest verses were prefixed to *The Poems of Henry Vaughan* in 1651, and of whom Aubrey records: 'Very good-natured; not at all high-minded; pretty fatt; not tall; red pumpled face; wrote out Verses in Innes, or Mottos in windowes, in her table-booke.'

*

An antonymic translation of *Old Possum's Book of Practical Cats* called *Impractical Dogs.*

*

Poetry readings. We take it for granted, today, that these are an essential part of poetry and the poetry scene, where we can experience poetry *live*, encounter new work straight from the author's mouth, ask the author questions afterwards, buy their books, network. Yet for Giacomo Leopardi, writing in the first half of the nineteenth century, 'reading or performing one's own compositions in front of others' was 'an ancient vice which was tolerable in previous centuries because it was rare, but which today, when everyone writes and it is very difficult to find someone who is not an author, has become a scourge, a public calamity'. The essence of Leopardi's argument is that, contrary to received opinion, work, even good work, is always destroyed when the author reads it themselves: 'Even the most beautiful and valuable writings, when their author is reciting them, become such as to kill with boredom.' In the style of the day, Leopardi backs up his argument with evidence from the classics: Octavia fainted when she heard Virgil read the sixth book of the *Aeneid* not because she was reminded of her son Marcellus, but through boredom; Martial hated public readings, and when asked by someone why he didn't read his verses to him replied, 'So as not to hear yours'; Diogenes the Cynic, finding himself at a poetry reading, caught sight of the blank page marking the end of the book that was in the reader's hands, and called out, 'Take heart, friends, I see land ahead'. The remarks still resonate today, and they remind me of a now legendary reading given by Tom Raworth at Essex University where, or so the story goes, following a lengthy set by Ted Berrigan and then Alice Notley (introduced by Berrigan with the words 'Alice is now going to read from her pregnancy poem', to which Raworth quipped 'Oh my God, this is going to take nine months!'), Raworth, when he was at last given the stage, stood up, read a one-liner, and sat down.

*

Shakespeare's sonnets have long been a source of inspiration for poets, who have returned to them again and again, emulating their dazzling combination of intricacy and duration, of feeling and colour, characterisation and the dramatisation of moods. They were the initial inspiration for Ted Berrigan's *The Sonnets* (1964), and K. Silem Mohammad, in *The Sonnograms* (2009), created a whole new sonnet sequence, in rhymed pentameter, by submitting Shakespeare's poems to a process of anagrammatisation. My own *Shakespeare's Sonnets* (2011) recreates the sonnet sequence from fragments of infotainment ideolects culled from the tabloid press, while in *Sleeping with the Dictionary* (2002), Harryette Mullen submits the sonnets to Oulipian procedures of N+7 to create wild refigurations of Shakespeare's forms and language. Another tradition in poetry, whose origins can perhaps be traced back to the synaesthesia of Rimbaud's poem 'Voyelles', where each vowel is assigned a colour – A black, E white, I red, U green, O blue – has explored colours in relation to poetry. The influence of Futurism and concrete poetry, as well as developments that have made the use of colour in print cheaper and more widely available, has led to coloured inks increasingly being employed in the *production* of poetry. Christian Bök, in one of several versions of 'Voyelles', translates the poem into bands of colour corresponding to those ascribed by Rimbaud to the vowels, and the French poet Jacques Roubaud has recently turned to the use of coloured inks in his poetry to add visual currents and clues to his complex polyphonic verse patternings. And the same can be said of the sometimes digitally inspired new concrete, as well as of visually inspired poetics more generally, as in the work of David Bellingham and André Vallias.

Armed with an interest in the new concrete and code poetry and a full spectrum of colours, Gregory Betts's *BardCode* – his second engagement with Shakespeare following his versions of sonnet 150 in *The Others Raisd in Me* (2009) – combines these until now separate traditions, by ascribing colours to the repeated sound patternings in Shakespeare's sonnets, calibrating the frequency of each sound pattern to the level of brightness, and printing off the resultant data visualisation in (mostly) 10 x 14 grids. The results are a series of 154 visual pieces, resembling expanded Rubic's cubes, or stained glass created by Mondrian or Paul Klee – Klee taught stained glass, bookbinding and mural workshops at the Bauhaus – that provide a map of the sonnets. At first glance, there's little to tell one of these visualisations from the next, but if we pay them attention they can tell us some things about Shakespeare's sonnets that might otherwise be overlooked. One thing they make instantly visible is the syllabic count of the sonnets, where Shakespeare's line veers into eleven or sometimes twelve syllables, and Betts's grid expands correspondingly, creating a penumbral border to the right-hand edges of the poems, foreshadowing the appearance of the 'dark lady' in sonnet 127 ('In the old age black was not counted fair'). Irregularity, the breaking of rules, in a word, is made visible, and when we reach sonnet 127 itself in *BardCode*, we are confronted by a love triangle of three irregularities in the shape of three misfit lines of eleven syllables each, echoing the irregularity that Shakespeare introduces into the conventions of the sonnet sequence at this point, by adding a new object of love who defies the sonneteer's stock range of epithets. Another thing that is highlighted in Betts's visualisations is something that we have perhaps known all along, but never articulated as clearly before, and this is that the music in Shakespeare's sonnets is not confined to the end-rhymes, but is there in every syllable of every poem, demonstrating how the sounds of the poems are literally orchestrated, making liberal use of internal rhyme and repetitive sound patternings and modulations of form and colour to weave their complex music. And this in turn lets us see why rhymed poetry often fails in lesser hands, for here the music is *only* there in the rhyme, and as such is too insistent, too obvious, like a sententious drum, as in the poems of Rudyard Kipling. This serves to remind us that if there is to be a future for rhymed poetry – as in the complex imbricated rhyming of Andrew Wynn Owen's *Infinite in Finite* (2023) – it needs to be in this direction.

*

When a young poet asks me for advice about writing poetry, and how to get better at writing poetry, I usually tell them to read as much as possible. That's what Ted Berrigan advised, and it makes sense to me, for to write you need to know what's being written, what other poets are up to, what it's possible to write today. It's also what I get from Michael Schmidt's *Lives of the Poets*, where he sketches so luminously how every poet is nourished by the poems of the past, whether that's Ted Hughes responding to Shakespeare, or Thom Gunn to Ben Jonson. Then, in Cowper's letters, I read: 'I reckon it among my principal advantages, as a composer of verses, that I have not read an English poet these thirteen years, and but one these twenty years. Imitation, even of the best models, is my aversion; it is servile and mechanical, a trick that has enabled many to usurp the name of author, who could not have written at all, if they had not written on the pattern of someone indeed original. But when the ear and the taste have been much accustomed to the manner of others, it is almost impossible to avoid it; and we imitate in spite of ourselves, just in proportion as we admire.'

*

There are poems that scholars will never find, ballads and lyrics, elegies, poems of moral precept, religious meditations, lives of saints... Were they lost because they weren't worth keeping, or because they were so constantly used that they were thumbed to pieces? Parchment wasted with the hungry love of reading eyes, recitation, with handing back and forth between poets and scholars and minstrels. Were they lost when, at the Reformation, great libraries were burned, or emptied out and sold to the local gentry – as the wicked and wonderful biographer and gossip John Aubrey remembers with pain – to be twisted into spills to start fires, or cut in convenient sheets as bog parchment (see, again, Michael Schmidt)?

*

When I think of sound poetry I think of names such as Bob Cobbing, Kurt Schwitters, Steve McCaffery, Tristan Tzara and Edwin Morgan, whose poem 'The Loch Ness Monster's Song' – beginning 'Sssnnnwhuf ff fll? / Hnwhuffl hhnnwfl hnfl hfl?' – was probably the first sound poem I came across, and which, in my teens, I turned into a song, singing the lines in a slightly deranged manner over acoustic guitar. But I think the first time I encountered something resembling sound poetry must have been in the womb, for we begin to hear in the womb after about eighteen weeks of pregnancy, and our hearing develops rapidly after that. What do we hear? We hear whatever is going on outside us, among which will be the voices of adults, muffled, lacking any sense, coming from another room we are shut off from and of which we know nothing, except for these muffled sounds which penetrate our space, no doubt mixed with the gurglings and whooshings of the internal organs. It strikes me that many sound poems, whatever else they are signifying, contain an echo of this originary misheard speech, jumbled up with 'organ music', whether by accident or design. I certainly hear something like this in Morgan's poem:

Grof grawff gahf?
Gombl mbl bl–
blm plm,
blm plm,
blm plm,
blp.

The first two lines sound like fragments of a half-heard conversation, the last four lines like the beating of a heart. And I think in this connecton of Julia Kristeva's 'semiotic chora' where the child, still undifferentiated from its environment, is infinitely open and connected to all that surrounds it, and I think too of Joyce's *Finnegans Wake* – Joyce is one of the writers championed in her book *Revolution in Poetic Language* – and it strikes me that the voices we hear, or half-hear, as we read, confusedly, the pages of *Finnegans Wake*, the greatest, certainly the longest, sound poem in the language – 'As he was soampling me ledder, like hulp, he'll fell the fall of me faus, he sazd, like yulp!' – are very like these voices we might half-hear in the womb, voices coming from another room, in a language we don't know.

*

Philip Larkin, writing in his Oxford College's library copy of Spenser's *The Faerie Queene*, scribbled: 'First I thought that *Troilus and Criseyde* was the most *boring* poem in English. Then I thought *Beowulf* was. Then I thought *Paradise Lost* was. Now I *know* that *The Faerie Queene* is the *dullest thing out. Blast it.*' Given Larkin's dislike of myth, and by analogy of epic, it's not hard to see why he would have found these works boring, particularly Spenser's poem, which so often leaves the everyday far behind. For a writer whose muse was boredom it may, however, also be true, at least in part, that these were paradoxically formative works. Larkin's dismissal of these poetic fables, for one thing, anticipates his poem 'A Study of Reading Habits', and its gleeful conclusion 'Books are a load of crap'. Then his poetics is almost the *opposite* of *The Faerie Queene*'s: Larkin adopts brevity, where Spenser has endlessly proliferating structures, Larkin writes plainly where Spenser writes fancifully, Larkin uses sparing metaphor, where Spenser develops multi-layered allegories. The one thing we find in Spenser which Larkin does not abandon (though he shares with Spenser an unabashed anglocentrism and the racism that goes hand in hand with it) is rhyme. In 'Church Going' – one of Larkin's poems conceived in Ireland, as I know from my mother who tells me that when she worked in Queen's University library, where Larkin was her boss, they encouraged him to visit some of the churches around Belfast – Larkin even pays homage to Spenser, adapting the Spenserian nine-line iambic stanza to his own needs.

*

We tend to think of poetry as a kind of perfection. But even the most gifted poets have off days. Wordsworth wrote some bad poems. Who hasn't? Walcott too. His 'A Country Club Romance' has an execrable extended metaphor revolving around tennis, which reaches its low point when Walcott uses the phrase 'Answer this backhand!' to describe the moment when a husband hits his wife. But such poems are still poetry, still part of poetry, and they remind us that poetry can fail, that poetry can be the record of a failed act of writing, the very opposite of Pope's definition of poetry: 'What oft was thought, but ne'er so well express'd'.

*

Poetry, ungraspable, prickly, always outstripping our definitions, nevertheless has definable functions, one of which is as a guardian of the word-hoard, even, as John Ashbery notes in his poem 'Palindrome', as guardian of 'Words / no dictionary ever knew, or even acknowledged having known, / like "spludge" or "parentitis"' – and 'parentitis', it turns out, is a key word for unpacking Ashbery's poem, whose palindromic structure begins with an infanticide and ends with the appearance of a child. Ashbery's interest in the word-hoard is echoed in the works of many poets. Paul Muldoon celebrates the word 'quoof' (his family's name for the hot water bottle), Heaney the word 'kesh' (a track raised above the wetness of a bog). Greg Thomas, in his collection *threshholds*, includes six proposals for *new* words, including 'underwhorl', 'rivert', and 'thinges', which combines the word 'things' with 'hinges', suggesting the way things connect to one another, and to us, rather than standing in isolation. The interest of poets in the word-hoard is shared by the writer Georges Perec, who in chapter sixty of his novel *Life a User's Manual*, introduces the character Cinoc, a 'word-killer', who works at keeping the Larousse dictionary up to date, not by seeking out new words and meanings, but by making room for them by eliminating words and meanings that have fallen into disuse. Among the hundreds and thousands of words eliminated by Cinoc are '*vigigraphe*' (a type of telegraph consisting of watchtowers communicating with each other), and '*velocimane*' (a locomotive device for children, resembling a horse, mounted on three or four wheels). In his retirement, Cinoc reverses the process, compiling a huge dictionary of forgotten words, such as '*pisteur*' (a hotel employee with the job of attracting new customers, a word which could usefully be introduced to the Higher Education sector today), and '*rondelin*' (a very fat man). The palindromic symmetry of the story echoes that of the central narrative of Perec's vast novel, where Bartlebooth paints landscapes which are made into jigsaws and then, having solved the puzzles, has the paintings destroyed. And there is every reason to see the Cinoc episode as occupying a central place in the novel, even encoding the title: Cinoc's obsolete words are *les mots vides d'emploi*, or words without any use, a Roussel-esque twist on the novel's French title, *La Vie mode d'emploi.* At the very heart of Perec's novel, then, we find two central elements of poetry: its function as a guardian of the word-hoard, and a riddle-like playing with language and sound, as in some of the most ancient poetry. And then, like Ashbery's poem, with its playful approach to structure, Perec shapes his novel according to the patterning of a palindrome. It is this which makes Perec's novel, or 'novels' as he puts it, a *poetic* novel, reminding us that poetry is not confined to poems, but can migrate into other modes and genres, popping up where we perhaps least expect to find it, in dictionaries, plotlines, lists, single words, and... novels.

*

Combinatory poetry has a long history, stretching back to the combinatorics of Ramon Llull's *Ars Magna* and the poetry of Jean Meschinot in the fifteenth century, but in modern times it owes its revival principally to Raymond Queneau, who in 1961 published a slim volume, inspired by the children's game *Heads, Bodies, Legs*, consisting of ten rhymed sonnets; and just as in that game body parts from each section can be interchanged, so any line in any one of these sonnets can replace the corresponding line in any other sonnet. The result, which proved to be an inaugural moment for the Oulipo – it remains one of the clearest examples of both 'potential literature' and 'combinatory literature' – was 10^{14} sonnets, or *Cent mille milliards de poèmes* (*A Hundred Thousand Billion Poems*). Almost ten years later, in 1970, Ted Berrigan published another slim volume, *In the Early Morning Rain*. It opens with '5 New Sonnets: A Poem', a disjunctive sonnet sequence, which turns out to be mechanically derived from Berrigan's 1964 book *The Sonnets*, taking line one of sonnet one, line two of sonnet two, line three of sonnet three and so on, to create five new sonnets. Berrigan's *The Sonnets* already works with the collaging and repositioning of fragments, but the work in the collection of 1970 brings his processes uncannily close to Queneau's on the other side of the Atlantic. There is no evidence that Queneau and Berrigan were aware of each other's work, but had they been, they would have found they had much in common, as does the Oulipian idea of constrained writing and the North American concept of procedural poetics, and, indeed, the work of the New York School in general. Asked in interview what the connection was between Oulipo and the New York School, Harry Mathews replied: 'There is no connection, except for me.' Mathews knew of at least one other connection, in Joe Brainard's *I Remember*, which he had described to Perec, and it was a form which was also picked up by Berrigan in a poem with the same title beginning 'I remember painting "I HATE TED BERRIGAN" in big black letters all over my white wall' (a line taken verbatim from Brainard). But beyond that there are other connections, in the work of John Ashbery, for example, who had revealed to Mathews the method of antonymic translation which became associated with Oulipo, and in the work of Ron Padgett, who had experimented with games involving noun substitution long before he became acquainted with Oulipo. This synchronicity between the interests of the New York School poets and those of the Oulipo can best be explained by their shared interests in the work of Duchamp and the French surrealists, and in the work of Oulipian anticipatory plagiarists such as Robert Desnos and Raymond Roussel. Raymond Berrigan's *Sonnets*, published by Joakim Norling's Timglaset Press in 2023, is a posthumous collaboration between these two seminal groups, Oulipo and the New York School, and between these two tireless experimenters, Berrigan and Queneau, which contributes to and continues the tradition of combinatorial poetry: it takes ten sonnets from Berrigan's *The Sonnets* and combines them with the structure of Queneau's collection to produce a trillion new sonnets, by Raymond Berrigan, of which this is just one:

The bulbs burn phosphorescent, white
my dream a crumpled horn
In the book of his music the corners have straightened:
'A fruitful vista, this, our South,' laughs Andrew to his Pa.
Dust has covered all the tacks, the hammer
A bright room, sustained by the darkness outside and
slow kisses on the eyelids of the sea,
ethereal, we are weird!   Each tree stands alone in stillness.
The bulbs burn phosphorescent, white
And the architecture.
had 17 and 1/2 milligrams
Poised like Nijinsky
Except at night. Then
I launched a boat as frail as a butterfly

Though perhaps even one trillion doesn't exhaust the possibilities here. At least since Borges's 'Pierre Menard, the Author of *Don Quixote*', we have known that to multiply authors is to multiply texts. And who is really the author here: is it Queneau or is it Berrigan, is it Raymond Berrigan, or is it Ted Queneau, or is it rather Oulipo, or is it someone else? And if it's all these, how many sonnets is that?

*

When a poem is ripe, it will fall. (Mallarmé)

Bibliography

Ashbery, John, *Can You Hear, Bird* (Manchester: Carcanet, 1996).

Aubrey, John, *Aubrey's Brief Lives*, ed. Oliver Lawson-Dick (London: Secker & Warburg, 1949).

Berrigan, Raymond, *Sonnets*, ed. Philip Terry (Malmö: Timglaset Editions, 2023).

Betts, Gregory, *BardCode* (Shrewsbury: Penteract Press, 2024).

Cowper, William, *William Cowper's Letters* (London: Oxford University Press, 1908).

Heaney, Seamus, *Seeing Things* (London: Faber and Faber, 1991).

Kristeva, Julia, *Revolution in Poetic Language*. transl. Margaret Waller (New York: Columbia University Press, 1985).

Larkin, Philip ed. *The Oxford Book of Twentieth Century English Verse* (London: Oxford University Press, 1973).

Leopardi, Giacomo, *Thoughts*, transl. J.G. Nichols (London: Hesperus Press, 2002).

Mallarmé, Stéphane, *Selected Poetry and Prose*, ed. Mary Ann Caws (New York: New Directions, 1982).
Muldoon, Paul, *Quoof* (London: Faber and Faber, 1983).
Mullen, Harryette, *Sleeping with the Dictionary* (Berkeley: University of California Press, 2002).
Murphy, Rosalie ed. *Contemporary Poets of the English Language* (London: St James Press, 1970).
Owen, Wilfred, *Collected Letters*, ed. Harold Owen and John Bell (London: Oxford University Press, 1967).
Perec, Georges, *Life a User's Manual*, transl. David Bellos (London: Harvill, 1988).
Schmidt, Michael, *Lives of the Poets* (London: Weidenfeld & Nicolson, 1998).
Thomas, Greg, *threshholds* (Malmö: Timglaset Editions, 2023).
Walcott, Derek, *In a Green Night* (London: Jonathan Cape, 1962).

Reviews

Begging Honey of the Sea

Vona Groarke, *Woman of Winter*, illustrations by Isabel Nolan (Gallery Books) €15
John Kinsella, *The Pastoraclasm* (Salt) £10.99
Reviewed by Gwyneth Lewis

On the face of it, these two books could not be more different: Vona Groarke's new version of the ninth-century poem *The Lament of the Hag of Beare*, a slim volume with its concise, seemingly straightforward quatrains and the sprawling eclogues and explicit ecological thinking of John Kinsella's *Pastoraclasm*. Yet both books address our contemporary moment with satire and archaeologies of deep time. They overlap content-wise in both writers' commitment to Ireland – see, for example, Kinsella's 'The Terrifying Prospect of Another Birdless Day, Indoors, Schull, West Cork', a title which is a poem in itself – but could not be more different in approach or method.

Groarke and Kinsella are both drawing on the root stock of ancient literature. Groarke's poem is a rendering of an anonymous poem spoken, as she says in her introduction, by a 'dramatic, articulate, wounded and resistant female protagonist'. The brief introduction explains that the hag/nun/ancestress figure blurs, by the eleventh century, into a mythic figure and is said to pass into 'seven periods of youth, so that every husband used to pass from her to death of old age, so that her grandchildren and great-grandchildren were peoples and races'.

Time behaves strangely around such figures and Groarke deftly ties her protagonist to her view of translation as a 'passing through'. She aims 'to write a new poem in contemporary English that draws upon the heritage of a poem' and she does so meticulously. This light touch has resulted in an exquisite, pitch-perfect rendition, giving us a poem that is utterly of our time. It's as if Groarke has struck an old, well-cast bell and found rich new overtones and resonances in its tone, capable of addressing our disturbing historical moment.

On the face of it, the poem is about the loss of status of the ageing woman. I laughed out loud at the opening stanza, in recognition:

> The tide has well and truly turned
> and not in my favour.
> But as much use to whinge about that
> As to beg honey of the sea.

This older woman speaks of youth in a psychologically recognizable way: 'All for money is the way of you lot. / Not so when I was young' and 'Full of the big talk these days are'. The only clumsy note for me was a reference to the topless feminist group Femen, because the rest of the poem deftly addresses the wider issues of misogyny and environmental degradation in its tone and this seemed too specific. Isabel Nolan has been equally allusive in giving us images drawn from old manuscripts but rendered in a fresh modern way. I could see Matisse, Picasso in her line drawings and she does a perfect greyhound (I know whereof I speak).

The old woman looks at the sea and its tides are central to its metre and view of history. 'Soldiers, horses, teeth-bared hounds' crash down on Ard Ruide Fort like waves. The speaker dwells on a world in decline: 'For the Yes of the incoming tide was ever / more pleasing to me than ebb's No'. This holds as much for the environment as it does for the inner tempering that old age brings. This spare and elegant version is an important addition to the historical voices from the Irish rendered to address the present.

John Kinsella's work has always engaged explicitly with environmental issues and *The Pastoraclasm* recounts lockdown gardening through the prism of the eclogue. The poet's drought-challenged garden provides the setting for a series of meditations on the biosphere and the pastoral genre. When seeds sell out during lockdown panic, the poet seeks out old packets of 'organic heirloom seeds, and these I sow'. So, too, he sows the eclogue and works with what emerges. Kinsella has always been alert to the moral trail left by literary forms and, of course, he interrogates the pastoral eclogue to see if it's an adequate vessel to describe contemporary environmental catastrophe. I didn't always follow these arguments (is he against the elegiac on principle?). He's certainly against anthropomorphism of nature and 'this grand Guignol / of pathetic fallacy' and yet, perhaps inevitably, he does it himself as, for example, in the image of a snake fleeing a fire 'anger in its eyes at your / belief that danger made you want and ceded / worlds within worlds to make them one'. And he's right to expose that, in the face of disastrous fires 'fire as propellant as literary device / of victory is false grammar'.

Kinsella is a thinking poet, and sets his ideas in the framework of long sequences at the scale of a whole book. This has its longueurs but he's capable of intense focus as well, as in the more traditional 'Rusticus Eclogue', a dialogue about a farmer who ruined another's organic crop by contaminating it with GM canola. If the dominant element of Groarke's vision of decline is water, fire is the god of Kinsella's book. The experience of reading it is like coming through a firestorm of ideas, to emerge, in the last poems, to a more streamlined vision, as in 'Eclogue of Fire', which is a dialogue between Soul and Self recast in a new theology. The Self remembers rain 'which vaporised / as it does now shown on the radar / before it even hits the ground'. This is a perfect balancing of political thinking with sensual detail. Some of the dialogues in earlier sequences sound like one speaker but here the voices become dramatically distinct as the poem proceeds, with the Self speaking in gorgeous images:

> Fire is beyond the senses. It reaches us before
> it is lit, before we perceive it, take it into sensibility.
> And yet, fire is the writer of the body's obituary.

The Soul's lines, in response, become shorter and end up with 'Fire makes / and takes stories. / Fire *gardens.*' The verb (which looks like a noun) overturns our human-centred view in one deft flip.

For me, Kinsella's shorter poems, such as 'Three Arguments with the Elements', give him a variety of tone that addresses his subject – 'all these ideas of contradictory *presence*' – more effectively. And yet, I can see that his interest in length and his ability to allow a form to have his way with him is another stance for wilderness in language, rather than willed profiting on a natural process, whether that be in the garden or on the page.

Highbrows

Robert Boyers, ***Maestros & Monsters: Days & Nights with Susan Sontag & George Steiner*** **(Mandel Vilar Press)**
£20.30
Reviewed by Tony Roberts

The life informs the work. *Tel arbre, tel fruit*, as Sainte-Beuve – likened to the author in a laudatory comment on the cover of the book under review – once wrote: *as with the tree, so with the fruit.* In many writers one feels this strongly. As the wonderfully incorrigible William Empson wrote, 'To say that you won't be bothered with anything but the words on the page (and that you are within your rights, because the author didn't *intend* you to have any more) strikes me as petulant... If you cared enough you would.'

How pleasing then, for like-minded readers, to chance on a well-written, insightful and affectionate memoir like Robert Boyer's *Maestro & Monsters*. And one is doubly fortunate because his subjects, Susan Sontag and George Steiner, were flamboyant intellectuals, major cultural critics of the '60s, that radical time when the distinction between 'high' and 'low' culture collapsed.

What they held in common, aside from being brilliant, Jewish, combative, admired and vilified (and alumni of the University of Chicago), was a relentless devotion to the written word, a profound seriousness, and an unremitting concern about the fortunes of culture. They were elitist (or grew to be in Sontag's case), both of them publicly indifferent to the hostility they generated by a whiff of superiority. More importantly, they brought to the attention of literary inclined readers in America and Europe the fruits of their readings in European culture. Ironically, the French-born Steiner could be scathing on American culture ('The Archives of Eden') and Sontag on America ('The America I live in is the America of the cities. The rest is just drive-through').

So they both looked to Europe. In the pages of the *Partisan Review* and the *New York Review of Books* Sontag championed filmmakers like Resnais, Bresson and Godard and such writers as Barthes, Walser and Weil. Her collections of essays were widely read: *Against Interpretation* (1966), with its rug-pulling title essay ('To interpret is to impoverish, to deplete the world – in order to set up a shadow world of "meanings"') and her Austinian 'Notes on "Camp"'); *On Photography* (1977); *Where the*

Stress Falls (2001); and *Illness as Metaphor* (1978), a work on critical theory. Steiner, a giant of comparative literature, promoted such writers as Adorno, Benjamin, Bernhard and Celan in the *New Yorker* and the *TLS*. His books included *Tolstoy or Dostoevsky* (1959), *The Death of Tragedy (1961)*, *In Bluebeard's Castle* (1971) and *After Babel* (1975).

Both writers looked with dismay at the direction culture had taken, Steiner from the first and Sontag in later years. In her *Paris Review* interview of 1994 she declared, 'taste has become so debauched in the thirty years I've been writing that now simply to defend the idea of seriousness has become an adversarial act... As you see, I'm chock-full of indignation about the barbarism and relentless vacuity of this culture.'

Her biographer, Benjamin Moser, noted that '[i]n the last decades of her life, it became hard to remember that she had once been considered a leveller. She came to symbolize high culture and the rigorous standards that upheld it.' In an interview of 2001 she clarified her position: 'In some sense I was as much a partisan or supporter of traditional cultural hierarchy as any cultural conservative, but I didn't draw the hierarchy in the same way.'

On his part, Steiner admitted in *Errata: An Examined Life* (1997) that 'the humanities do not humanise, that the sciences, and even philosophy can serve the worst of politics'. Yet in spite of that, '[i]t happens to be blindingly obvious to me that study, theological-philosophic argument, classical music, poetry, art, all that is "difficult because it is excellent" are the excuse for life.'

There were, of course, great differences between their areas of interest and the approach the two took. Sontag, the more radical, offered celebrity and activism (in Vietnam, in Sarajevo); Steiner, polymath and pedagogue, travelled the international university circuits. Unsurprisingly we learn that they 'disliked and mistrusted one other' on the few occasions they met.

What they were like off their soap boxes we learn from *Maestros & Monsters*. Boyers is an academic, editor and founder of the quarterly *Salmagundi*. His admiration for both, despite frequent provocations, wins over the reader. He has, as a friend told him, a 'gift for admiration' and yet he is also unillusioned about their reputations:

> George was never entirely forgiven by some for the theatricality of his pronouncements, the want of sobriety, the breadth of his reach. To her detractors, Susan seemed almost comical in the extremity of her ardor and the presumption of authority that informed her writing. [...] Like Steiner, she sometimes worked 'outward from the particular literary instance to the far reaches of moral and political arguments,' as George himself put it.

Maestros & Monsters takes each writer in turn. Moser, in *Sontag: Her Life* (2019), gave us the sound, the disorder and the fury of Sontag. Boyers illustrates some of the same by way of anecdotal revelations concerning her behaviour in his company, which was often rude and demanding. He also examines his own motivation in befriending Sontag. After admiring her brilliance and the electricity of her presence, he acknowledges that he was compensated by the attention she paid to him and his wife, Peg, and to *Salmagundi*. At one point he writes, '[p]rincipally, I felt in my sense of Susan as an authority figure that I must labor to be worthy of the interest she took in me.'

He also writes informatively about her prose. A provocateur, there were times when she wrote nonsense. So, when trashing the notion of the 'nuclear' family in 'The Third World of Women', 'she was not earnestly contending for plausibility and reasonableness but giving herself permission to be excessive, brash, peremptory'. At times, he suggests, she was simply attracted to the raw newness of the new, and he wonders at her readiness to 'aestheticize' without due thought. Crucially, he recognises that '[s]he wrote, for the most part, not to instruct but to declare an interest.'

With George Steiner the same method applies. He could be demanding, hard in his expectations of students – Boyers was one – brusque and abrasive in person, but also gregarious and fascinating: 'I admired his drive, his erudition, his work ethic, and I was grateful he saw something admirable in me'. Like Sontag he was a friend to the Boyerses and to the magazine. Unlike her, Steiner wrote to instruct his readers.

His bouts of humility thrilled Boyers: He could be 'frank about the degree to which his own generative insights [were] rooted in hypotheses open to dispute'. He could be humble in his calling (a self-described 'courier' from the arts) and yet he took intellectual 'risks' in his writing, which took him outside his specialisms.

If Steiner lacked Sontag's celebrity, he could nevertheless fill large lecture halls and thrill his audiences. If anecdotes about him lack a little of the colour of hers, we nevertheless gain some insight into his controversies. Boyers devotes time to contextualising insults by Edward Said and by Sontag herself, and he defends Steiner against unjust comments by James Wood (for whom he declares great admiration).

Maestros & Monsters is an entertaining read by a veteran critic and a hopelessly long-suffering fan. It also offers, *inter alia*, a buried reading list. I wonder what its ticklish subjects would have thought of the title?

A Gesture of Disgust

Richard Aldington, *Exile and Other Poems*, with introduction and notes by Elizabeth Vandiver and Vivien Whelpton (Renard Press) £10
Reviewed by John Greening

Richard Aldington (1892–1962) is most often remembered for his biographies and memoirs or for his relationship with the poet H.D.; his own poetry tends to be overlooked by critics and anthologists, something he lamented in a characteristically crotchety introduction to his 1948 *Complete Poems*. He certainly wouldn't have been pleased to find himself excluded from Tim Kendall's landmark *Poetry of the First World War* (Oxford, 2013). If he has lacked a popular following, it may be because the work has yet to reach enough readers; or perhaps because – witness the title poem of *Exile* (1923) – it still betrays that intrusive 'anger and bitterness' noted by Edmund Blunden (in a *TLS* review quoted by the editors) which leads him into 'gestures of disgust which do not belong to the poet in him'. Although he had published a good deal before this collection, according to his editors it is his 'first substantial attempt to process the trauma of his experience in poetry'. That trauma was chiefly the First World War, which shaped and marred both the man and the work, but it is also a dysfunctional family background and the stillbirth of the child he had with Hilda. This new edition, beautifully produced by Renard for Aldington's centenary, would be worth having just for the first-rate introduction and the detailed background notes which give a very clear summary of his troubles.

Setting those aside, the poetry is enjoyable within the limitations of Aldington's self-obsessed and determinedly unlyrical style. There is an arresting realism and his lines on nature have a Lawrentian drive (he wrote significant biographies of both D.H. and T.E.) but it is strange that this Imagist should be so ill-attuned to imagery. Nevertheless, the stark, journalistic manner can be effective and might be regarded as more truthful:

> Loos, that horrible night in Hart's Crater,
> The damp cellars of Maroc,
> The frozen ghostly streets of Vermelles,
> That first night-long gas bombardment –
> O the thousand images I see
> And struggle with and cannot kill –
> That boot I kicked
> (It had a mouldy foot in it)
> The night K.'s head was smashed
> Like a rotten pear by a mortar [...]
> (from 'Eumenides')

But then one thinks of what Isaac Rosenberg or Robert Graves did with similar scenes – or indeed of Wilfrid Gibson's home-spun (and wholly imagined) battle verse. *Exile* is not all about war, but its presence looms. 'Rhapsody in a Third-Class Carriage', for instance, is a snapshot of an ungrateful and 'mediocre' post-war England of pianolas and hobnails.

By contrast, the book's unexpected and refreshing second part, 'Words for Music', consists of some rather brilliant homages to seventeenth-century love poets along with two pastoral 'Metrical Exercises'. *Exile* in fact features several formal pieces, including a version of Villon and epigrammatic squibs such as 'Those Who Played for Safety in Life'. It has to be said that Richard Aldington feels more at home here and is evidently enjoying the chance to sing. Perhaps he was never really an Imagist at all.

Contact with the Now

Hélio Oiticica, *Secret Poetics*, translated by Rebecca Kosick with essays by Rebecca Kosick and Pedro Erber (Soberscove Press and Winter Editions) $24
Reviewed by Greg Thomas

One of the most charming of the 'secret poems' by the Brazilian artist Hélio Oiticica (1937–80) included in this new edition of translations by Rebecca Kosick reads as follows:

> Water,
> glassy surface,
> plunge.

The reader put in mind of Bashō's famous 'frog/pond/plop' haiku (that hyper-compact translation from Dom

Sylvester Houédard) might well be on the money. As Kosick points out in her introduction, '[w]e don't know for sure that a reference to Bashō was deliberate, but we know haiku is a form Oiticica was working with at this time'.

However, as Kosick goes on to note, readers familiar with Oiticica's oeuvre might also sense in this poem from 1964 a pre-emptive linguistic rendering of his artwork *Plunge of the Body* (1966–7). Reproduced in Kosick's book, this consists of a water-filled basin with the title-words 'Mergulho do corpo' inscribed on its bottom-surface, facing the viewer like an invitation to a physical act. (Many of Oiticica's 1960s artworks solicited physical interaction.)

Then again, there is a level of abstraction to Oiticica's language that resists both readings just offered. The absence of any tangible, naturalistic subject matter (like a frog and a pond, say, or a body and a basin) almost seems to nudge it into the realms of metaphysical speculation. It's as if the unbounded, unlocated body of water, and the plunge undertaken by an unnamed subject or object, are metaphors for more general states of being, feeling or knowing.

These divergent readings give a flavour of the manifold resonances of Oiticica's *Secret Poetics*, a sequence created irregularly during 1964–6. Kosick discovered the little cache of verses during research for an earlier book, fronted by two prose pieces that offered hints of method and motive: 'I am not a poet, although an urgent necessity leads me to poetic expression'; '[t]he true lyric is immediate, that is, immediacy that becomes eternal in lyrical poetic expression'.

The period when *Secret Poetics* was written was one of violent transition for Brazil. A right-wing military dictatorship seized power in 1964 and maintained it for the next twenty-one years. It was also a time of transformation in Oiticica's personal life. He was coming to terms with his sexuality, and his first gay romantic encounters date to this period, possibly to 1964 when, as Pedro Erber notes in a second essay included in the book, 'he took up dancing and started participating in the samba scene in Mangueira, a favela on the northern side of Rio [de Janeiro, Oiticica's home city]'.

Oiticica is internationally recognised as an artist but not as a poet: so what is the value and function of these works? Partly, as Kosick points out, they appeal as 'documents of a contemporary artist's developing ideas and thinking'. There is also a strongly phenomenological bent to the writing which gives an interesting sense of the intellectual discourse within the neo-concrete art movement to which Oiticica was attached. Passages such as 'The smell, / new touch, / restarting of the senses, / absorption, / memory, / oh!' suggest an attempt to somehow immaculately transcribe or preserve the felt moment of writing, with Maurice Merleau-Ponty a particular reference-point, as Erber states.

But most engagingly, as records of the embodied moment, these poems encode the feelings of desire, lust, pain and confusion animating the writing sensorium: 'Black skin, / contact with the now, / vision of the always, / love; // dark, / vision of the tactile, contact. // velvet, / caress of the touch, / the always in the always, / embrace // the arm, / body and I interlace, / lip'. These secret poems are documents of a mind and body realising themselves in loving and lustful relation to others at a time of personal and sociopolitical turmoil.

Living through the Fire

Marjorie Lotfi, *The Wrong Person To Ask* (Bloodaxe)
£10.99
Reviewed by Verak Yuen

The Wrong Person To Ask is Marjorie Lotfi's debut poetry collection. These tender and intricate poems chart a journey across continents, chronicling a childhood of unrest and violence in Iran and the nuances of relocation to America and Scotland. Lotfi's work interweaves the personal with the national, illuminating past and present tragedies through the quotidian rhythms of a new existence abroad.

Lotfi's verse is filled with directives, as if to guide readers through a terrain crowded with exploding mortars and crumbling buildings. Nothing is too sacred to be destroyed in an instant, and resistance could seem futile, evident in 'Refuge', an ekphrastic poem:

> Take out
> his thighs, but leave
> his knees to buckle
> at kindness, and the lack
> of it. Don't loosen his grip
> on the suitcase; it holds
> all he owns. Instead, nail
> his feet to the planks
> of the pier and let him try
> to take another step.

The poem takes its inspiration from Frances Bruno Catalano's *Les Voyageurs* sculpture, and the verse, too, has a hollowed-out quality. The line breaks are choppy but decisive and the brevity of Lotfi's diction conveys an immense sense of loss. *What more can this poem be alluding to? What more is left unsaid?* The plosives of 'take', 'buckle', 'grip' and 'planks' hammer into listeners' ears and jolt them into alertness. 'Hope' is written in a similar style to 'Refuge', both of which are generous with their use of imperatives. This time, each stanza starts with a commanding verb: 'Strip it off', 'Carry only' and 'Curl into', highlighting the necessity of becoming unencumbered on the journey ahead, as well as the importance of human connections and closeness.

It is the method her poems play out in ordinary settings that render them striking and memorable. 'Alarm II' takes place in an American middle school, but there are remnants of the battleground that resound in the speaker's mind:

> We live through the fire, and years
> later practise our safe escape,
> before the Principal announces
> on the loudspeaker in every class
> that today's exercise was only
> a drill, that we'd done it well.

Taking refuge has become so Pavlovian that instinct compels the speaker and their classmates, when the alarm goes off, to 'drop to our knees / like folding onto a prayer mat. Each / of us freezes in the brace position.' The matter-of-fact tone gives the impression that these children are mature beyond their age as a result of their experience of calamity. 'Alarm II' is a companion to 'Alarm I', which is set in Tehran years earlier and lends weight and context to the latter poem:

> Suddenly,
> each of us knows this Revolution,
> its pyre quietly built in the corner
> of sight, and all we'd done to set it
> alight was open our mouths.

Language has the power to build and destroy, and Lotfi wastes no words carving out in a bas-relief the incongruity of children learning Farsi at school and the experience of warfare around the corner. The poem ends on an uncertain and almost passive note, foreshadowing the years of trepidation and guilt that follows as Lotfi makes her home abroad.

The latter poems in Lotfi's collection explore notions of belonging and the right to tell one's story when re-situated in a vantage point of safety. The sentiment of the title poem, 'The Wrong Person To Ask', is echoed by 'The End of the Road', which is made up of vignettes from the speaker's daily life. There is an elegiac quality to her diction: 'There's a moment every morning / when she forgets – opens her mouth / to her mother tongue and finds / the silence foreign'. The vignettes that follow are quotidian but somehow crystalline and precious, perhaps alluding to the fragility of peace and the ease with which it has been shattered in the past. There is homesickness and lamentation, as memories and experiences retreat back in the rearview mirror.

Lotfi's poems exist in conversation with other poets with Palestinian roots such as Naomi Shihab Nye and Mahmoud Darwish. Her work share similarities too with Mosab Abu Toha's collection *Things You May Find Hidden in My Ear: Poems from Gaza*, as both deal with belonging in a brutalized homeland and give voice to the unspeakable as well as the beautiful: interrogating language, identity, loss and the resilience of Palestinians and Iranians in the face of war and displacement.

Ghosts on the Page

Safiya Kamaria Kinshasa, *Cane, Corn & Gully* (Out-Spoken Press) £11.99
Reviewed by Jazmine Linklater

Cane, Corn & Gully is multifaceted and hugely ambitious, especially for a first collection. A staunchly feminist project of decolonial counterhistory, it refuses linear time and speaks various kinds of language. Safiya Kamaria Kinshasa has developed a fascinating interdisciplinary mode of research-based creative production.

I think the best word to describe this poetry is haunted. Its major work is reckoning with how the past exists in and creates the present. And at its heart is a doomed desire: to recover and hear the stories of enslaved Barbadian women. But we are all too familiar with the silences which emanate from the archives, and in her research Kinshasa 'could not find a single word from an enslaved woman in Barbados'. Before she was a poet, however, Kinshasa was a dancer, and it was by attending to movement as a nonverbal, bodily mode of communication that the archives began to yield hidden narratives. Looking specifically for records of people moving, she 'discovered the enslaved people were speaking, constantly'. Kinshasa is candid about how 'the work is dangerous', because going back over the historical accounts of slavery is to consume once more the enslaver's narrative in the enslaver's voice. But she was driven: 'I was certain if I focused on the fundamental actions, I could loosen the gaze whose teeth marks can be found on my own anatomy.' Her turn of phrase is beautiful even when navigating dreadful complexity.

Admittedly, Kinshasa's methodology is unclear. By re-enacting enslaved people's documented movements, she accesses 'the discourse of their narratives' – necessarily nonverbal and heavily mediated. It seems inherently mysterious, a sort of shamanic receiving of language through ritualised movement. I wonder what it must feel like in her body. She brings ghosts through her and onto the page and imagines them speaking. Does this process free the movements from the colonial narrative by which they are preserved? It certainly makes them travel – from layered processes of translation they emerge as many different kinds of language: verbal, vernacular, visual, notative, gestural, bodily.

Throughout the book are hand-drawn 'Phrases', choreography scores transcribed in Labanotation, alongside 'Notes', short poetic texts which may or may not be verbal translations of the movements. These drawings are beautiful – circular, repetitive, with visual rhymes of density and negative space. There's a key, but for the untrained eye it's impossible to decipher how the score might be produced as human movement. Which is, I think, part of the point. Its inclusion contributes to the book's commitment to heterogeneity – not only different kinds of language but different kinds of knowledge and modes of transmission, navigating different levels of communicability and comprehensibility, which will shift around with different readers. There are many monologues here, for example, that are spoken in local vernacular, heavily accented, joyfully refusing the colonial language of standardised English.

Elsewhere language is totally redacted, leaving only titles and punctuation marks dotted across otherwise blank pages, like in 'Slow Whine'. I've been reading these redactions as acts of solidarity with the enslaved people whose voices are missing from the archives. Because Kinshasa's project is ultimately not one of recovery but invention – and these redacted poems remind us of the reality that these stories do not exist in the historical accounts. By recreating a void where there should be a narrative and holding it up for us to look at, she acknowledges the impossibility of her project alongside our shared, unfulfillable desires to hear these women speak.

Sometimes the poems are actually haunted, by the phantoms and jumbies of West Indian ghost stories and their surreally nightmarish images, like when 'now a duppy is bathing in my mouth'. Sometimes the speakers are haunted by contemporary pop culture and the ways in which western beauty standards simultaneously exoticize and exclude Black women. But it's often the more metaphorical haunting which is the most visceral, like in 'I Salted de Mud With My Palms But More ah Me Grew', a breath-taking poem spoken by someone forced to work in the sugar cane plantations: 'if i hang myself tonight, / tomorrow i will be back in de field / hundreds ah me to de left / to de right front back / every diagonal above below'.

The book acknowledges over and over again that the past imbues every present moment. Timelines are merged and overlaid, with many poems taking place in two distinct but connected historical moments, like in 'Behind de Garrison' which is set in both 1795, the year the West India Regiment was established, and 1975, when Queen Elizabeth II visited the island. Elsewhere narratives emerge from events relayed in colonial texts from the eighteenth and nineteenth centuries. A list of 'Key Informants & Agitators' in the notes includes titles like *Memoirs of a Slave Trader* and author names like 'Griffith Hughes'.

There is violence and pain and inherited trauma in this book. But there is also joy and playfulness – while some poems are certainly autobiographical, every poem that isn't is spoken by a different character. I love that some of the 'Phrases' are provided by 'Guest Choreographers', including 'The Afro Comb' and 'The Bearded Fig Tree'. There's one really weird moment where an enslaved woman speaks from within an Englishman's throat, 'riding the bacterium causing tonsilitis' that resides there while he's ostensibly giving a speech on abolishing slavery, and somehow Kinshasa manages to make this an impressively powerful poem. Sometimes I had more reservation about her speakers and wasn't sure what motivated the decision to ventriloquise a plantation owner who already had, and continues to have, so much capacity for speech. But these misgivings were minor. I found *Cane, Corn & Gully* expansive, unsettling, and hugely endearing.

Some Contributors

John Aberdein has taught and lived between Stromness and Hoy since 1983. His novel *Amande's Bed* received the Saltire First Book Award in 2005. Its sequel *Strip the Willow* was adjudged Fiction of the Year by the Scottish Arts Council in 2010. **Rowland Bagnall**'s first collection, *A Few Interiors*, was published by Carcanet in 2019. His poems, reviews and essays have appeared in *Poetry London*, *PN Review*, *The Art Newspaper* and the *Los Angeles Review of Books*. *Near-Life Experience*, his second book, is due in 2024. https://www.rowlandbagnall.com/. **Duncan Forbes**'s poems have been published by Faber, Secker and Enitharmon, who brought out a *Selected Poems* in 2009, drawn from five previous collections. His most recent collection is *Human Time* 2020. He read English at Oxford and has taught for many years. **Jamie McKendrick**'s most recent publications are *The Years*, a self-illustrated pamphlet of poems, and a book of writings on poetry and art, *The Foreign Connection.* **Philip Terry** was born in Belfast, and is a poet and translator. Carcanet published his edition of Jean-Luc Champerret's *The Lascaux Notebooks*, the first ever anthology of Ice Age poetry, in 2022. The Trinidadian Scottish writer **Anthony V. Capildeo** FRSL OPL is Writer in Residence at the University of York. *Polkadot Wounds* (Carcanet, 2024) is their ninth full-length book of poetry. **Robert Griffiths** is a poet and philosopher. He has published poems and articles in magazines. He can be found at *www.robertgriffiths.net*. **Lucy Sheerman**'s first collection of poems, *Pine Island*, an experimental memoir written in the form of a series of letters to an unknown recipient, was published by Shearsman Books in September 2023. **Tony Roberts** has had five collections of poetry. His third collection of essays, *A Movement of Mind* – on twentieth-century poets and Victorian biographers – will be published by Shoestring Press in September. **Gwyneth Lewis** was Wales's first National Poet. She wrote the inscription on the front of the Wales Millennium Centre, now in six-foot-high letters. She writes in both Welsh and English. Her memoir Nightshade Mother: *A Distetangling* is forthcoming this year. **Maria Stepanova** is a poet, essayist and the author of *In Memory of Memory* (Fitzcarraldo Editions, 2020). Her most recent poetry collection *Holy Winter 20/21* is published by Bloodaxe Books in Spring 2024. **Sasha Dugdale**'s sixth work of poetry *The Strongbox* is forthcoming from Carcanet in May 2024. **Spencer Hupp** is a poet and critic from Little Rock, Arkansas. His work has run in the *Sewanee Review*, *Raritan*, the *Los Angeles Review of Books*, the *Times Literary Supplement*, among others. He currently serves as a research fellow at Johns Hopkins University, where he took his MFA in 2022. **Jena Schmitt**'s poetry, short fiction, essays and drawings have appeared in publications in Canada, the US. and the UK. Her interests include writing about writers, artists and writer-artists. She lives in Sault Ste. Marie, Ontario, Canada, with her children. **Wayne Hill** made a quarter-mile musical instrument (it took him six years) after someone stole one of his smaller sculptures from an exhibition. He was once struck by lightning. **Stav Poleg**'s debut poetry collection, *The City* (Carcanet, 2022) was chosen for the *Financial Times*' Best Summer Books 2022, and was shortlisted for the Seamus Heaney Poetry Prize for a First Collection, 2023. Her poetry has appeared on both sides of the Atlantic, in the *New Yorker*, *Kenyon Review*, *Poetry Ireland Review*, *PN Review* and elsewhere. A selection of her work is featured in *New Poetries VIII* (Carcanet, 2021). **Vera K. Yuen** is a poet residing in London, where she is an undergraduate at Royal Holloway. Due to her diverse upbringing in Hong Kong and the West, she is interested in writing about culture, language and transformation in both internal and external worlds. She is the 2022 winner of the Charles Causley International Poetry Competition and is highly commended in the Disabled Poets Prize 2023. She is also a current Barbican Young Poet.

Editors
Michael Schmidt
John McAuliffe

Editorial Manager
Andrew Latimer

Contributing Editors
Anthony Vahni Capildeo
Sasha Dugdale
Will Harris

Copyeditor
Maren Meinhardt

Designed by
Andrew Latimer

Editorial address
The Editors at the address on the right. Manuscripts cannot be returned unless accompanied by a stamped addressed envelope or international reply coupon.

Trade distributors
Combined Book Services Ltd

Represented by
Compass IPS Ltd

ISBN 978-1-80017-419-1
ISBN 0144-7076

Subscriptions—6 issues
INDIVIDUAL–print and digital: £45; abroad £65
INSTITUTIONS–print only: £76; abroad £90
INSTITUTIONS–digital only: from Exact Editions (https://shop.exacteditions.com/gb/pn-review)
to: PN Review, Alliance House, 30 Cross Street, Manchester, M2 7AQ, UK.

Supported by